WORSHIP PLANNING
RESOURCES FOR
EVERY SUNDAY OF THE YEAR

The

Abingdon Worship
Annual 2021

✦

Edited by
Mary Scifres
and B. J. Beu

Abingdon Press / Nashville

The Abingdon Worship Annual 2021

WORSHIP PLANNING RESOURCES
FOR EVERY SUNDAY OF THE YEAR

Copyright © 2020 by Abingdon Press

ISBN 978-1-5018-9665-1

20 21 22 23 24 25 26 27 28 29—10 9 8 7 6 5 4 3 2 1

MANUFACTURED IN THE UNITED STATES OF AMERICA

Contents

CONTENTS

September

October

November

December

Introduction

The worship landscape has changed so much over the past twenty years that worship leaders are feeling overwhelmed. Many church pastors and worship leaders find themselves faced with expectations to match the quality and polish of mega churches with their vast resources and talent pool. Today's pastors and worship leaders understand that worship planning is a sacred undertaking that is both joyous and sobering. And they understand that, for many people, worship is the only activity that leads them into an awareness of God's presence in their lives.

With expectations for quality worship on the rise, it would be wonderful if church staff and volunteers had un-interrupted time each week to devote to worship planning. Sadly, our schedules often leave us little choice but to fit it in among the myriad tasks and responsibilities placing demands on our time. This problem becomes even more pronounced when worship leaders are faced with demands for diverse music and worship styles, and eye-catching on-screen presentations. Add in multimedia, visuals, texting, tweeting, and visitors "liking" your church on Facebook (during worship), and the pressures placed upon worship planners can become overwhelming.

This is where *The Abingdon Worship Annual 2021* becomes invaluable as a resource and partner in your planning process. In this resource, we provide theme ideas and all the written and spoken elements of worship, following the Revised Common Lectionary. *The Abingdon Worship Annual 2021* offers words for worship that provide the framework for congregations to participate fully in the liturgical life of worship.

In *The Abingdon Worship Annual 2021*, you will find the words of many different authors, poets, pastors, laypersons, and theologians. Some authors have written for this resource before; others provide a fresh voice. Since the contributing authors represent a wide variety of denominational and theological backgrounds, their words will vary in style and content. Feel free to combine or adjust the words within these pages to fit the needs of your congregation and the style of your worship. (Notice the reprint permission for worship given on the copyright page of this book.)

Each entry provides suggestions that follow an order of service that may be adapted to address your specific worship practice and format. Feel free to reorder or pick and choose the various resources to fit the needs of your worship services and congregations. Each entry follows a thematic focus arising from one or more of the week's scriptures.

To fit the Basic Pattern of Christian Worship—reflecting a flow that leads from a time of gathering and praise, into a time of receiving and responding to the Word, and ending with a time of sending forth—each entry includes Centering Words, Call to Worship and Opening Prayer, Prayer of Confession and Words of Assurance, Response to the Word, Offering Prayer, and Benediction. Communion Resources are offered in selected entries. Additional ideas are also provided throughout this resource.

Some readers find the Centering Words (also known as Contemporary Gathering Words or Unison Prayers) useful

printed in a worship handout or projected on a screen. Use
the words offered here in the way the best suits your congregation's spiritual needs, and please remember to give
copyright and author credit!

Using the Worship Resources

Calls to Worship gather God's people together as they
prepare to worship. Often called "Greetings" or "Gathering
Words," these words may be read by one worship leader or be
read responsively. Regardless of how they are printed in this
resource, feel free to experiment in your services of worship.
They may be read antiphonally (back and forth) between two
readers or two groups within the congregation: women and
men, choir and musicians, young people and old, and so on.

Opening Prayers in this resource are varied in form but
typically invoke God's presence into worship. Whether for-
mal, informal, general, or specific, these prayers serve to
attune our hearts and minds to God. Although many may
be adapted for use in other parts of the worship service, we
have grouped them into the category "Opening Prayers."

Prayers of Confession and **Words of Assurance** lead the
people of God to acknowledge our failing while assuring us
of God's forgiveness and grace. Regardless of how they are
printed, whether unison or responsively, Prayers of Confession and Words of Assurance may be spoken by a single
leader or led by a small group. Some prayers may even be
used as Opening or Closing Prayers.

Litanies and **Responsive Readings** offer additional av-
enues of congregational participation in our services of
worship. Think creatively as you decide how to use these

Responsive Readings in your service of worship: in unison, by a worship leader alone, or in a call and response format. Feel free to change the title of these liturgies to suit your worship setting.

Benedictions, sometimes called "Blessings" or "Words of Dismissal," send the congregation forth to continue the work of worship. Some of these Benedictions work best in call and response format; others work best when delivered as a blessing by a single worship leader. As always, use the format best suited to your congregation.

In response to requests from many of our readers, we have provided a number of **Communion** liturgies as well, each written specifically to relate to the thematic and scriptural focus of the day. Some follow the pattern of the Great Thanksgiving; others are Invitations to Communion or Prayers of Consecration for the celebration of the Eucharist.

Although you will find *The Abingdon Worship Annual 2021* an invaluable tool for planning worship, it is but one piece of the puzzle for worship preparation. For additional music suggestions, you will want to consult *Prepare! An Ecumenical Music and Worship Planner*, or *The United Methodist Music and Worship Planner*. These resources contain lengthy listings of lectionary-related hymns, praise songs, vocal solos, and choral anthems.

As you begin your worship planning, read the scriptures for each day, then meditate on the **Theme Ideas** suggested in this resource. Review the many words for worship printed herein and listen for the words that speak to you. Trust God's guidance, and enjoy a wonderful year of worship and praise!

Mary Scifres and B. J. Beu, Editors
The Abingdon Worship Annual
beuscifres@gmail.com

January 1, 2021

New Year's Day

Joanne Carlson Brown

Color

White

Scripture Readings

Ecclesiastes 3:1-13; Psalm 8; Revelation 21:1-6a;
Matthew 25:31-46

Theme Ideas

This is a time of new beginnings—a time to reflect on the
promises of newness and possibilities. God is making all
things new. It is also a time to reflect on the fact that there
is a time for everything under heaven. We are called to
renew our covenant with God—the covenant to be the
people God calls us to be; to be God's hands and feet in
the world; and to bring the message that in God's realm,
there is comfort, love, justice, and a chance to begin anew.

Invitation and Gathering

Centering Words (Eccl 3)
This is the day of new beginnings. Today, God dwells
with us. Today, all things are made new.

Call to Worship (Eccl 3)

For everything there is a season.

We come to worship God with our whole lives.

We celebrate all the times of our lives:

times to laugh and dance,

times to cry and mourn,

times of silence and times of speech,

times of war and times of peace.

Come let us worship the God of our times and seasons.

–Or–

Call to Worship (Ps 8)

Come, people of God.

Come and worship our God.

How majestic is your name in all the earth.

Come, people of God.

Come and worship the God who cares for us.

We give thanks to our loving and caring God.

Come, people of God.

Come and worship the God who crowns us

with glory and honor.

We celebrate the God of glory and wonder.

Proclamation and Response

Opening Prayer

Ever loving God, we come to a new year

with hopes and dreams, fears, and doubts.

As we step across the threshold of this new year,

may we have confidence in your abiding presence

in all the myriad aspects of our lives.

Open us to all, in this time of worship,

the possibilities and promises a new year can bring.

Bring your new heaven and new earth,
> that we may live with you in justice and peace.

We pray this in the name of God,
> the alpha and omega,
>> the one of new beginnings. Amen.

Prayer of Confession (Matt 25)

Ever present, ever loving God,
> we come to this new year
>> mindful of the things we have done
>> and left undone in the past.

Forgive the times when we did not reach out in love
> to the least of your sons and daughters.

Forgive us, O God,
> when we closed our eyes
>> to the sight of people
>>> living in rags on the street;
> when we stopped our ears
>> to cries of those who are lonely;
> when we turned away from the sight
>> of swollen, malnourished bodies.

Help us to see you in all we meet.

Help us to be your hands, feet, and voice in this world.

May we work for a world
> where no one will be a stranger,
>> and where all will be welcomed
>>> into your eternal glory. Amen.

Words of Assurance (Matt 25)

Our God is a God of compassion and love,
> ready to forgive all who truly repent
> and desire to live a life of justice and love.

Know that the God who calls us
to be members of God's family,
will welcome you with open arms
of grace and forgiveness.

Response to the Word (Ps 8)

Majestic is God's name in all the earth!
Praise to God, the sovereign of all,
who offers us the words that lead to life.
Praise our caring and creating God,
who fills us with glory and honor.

Thanksgiving and Communion

Offering Prayer (Eccl 3)

O God of all seasons and purposes under heaven,
we come in this season of new beginnings
to pray for guidance
in all the aspects of our lives.
Help us to remember that no matter what happens,
you are always with us—
in times of joy and sadness, life and death,
silence and speech, dancing and mourning,
war and peace.
May our lives reflect the glory to your name.
As we are mindful of the past,
let us rejoice in the future.
We pray in the name of the God
of all of our days and ways. Amen.

Sending Forth

Benediction (Eccl 3)

Go forth, rejoicing that our God is with us
in all times and places,
and in all the seasons of our lives.

–Or–

Benediction (Rev 21)

Go forth into the new year, trusting in God's promises.
And may God, the alpha and the omega,
be with you always.

January 3, 2021

Epiphany of the Lord
Joanne Carlson Brown

Color

White

Scripture Readings

Isaiah 60:1-6; Psalm 72:1-7, 10-14; Ephesians 3:1-12;
Matthew 2:1-12

Theme Ideas

In the Northern Hemisphere, we are experiencing the
darkness of midwinter. Days are short and nights long.
But there are other forms of darkness—poverty, war, injustice, oppression, hatred, prejudice, fear—forms that
also affect us just as they did the people of biblical times.
But in these passages, light breaks through the darkness:
a prophet calls us to arise and see the light of liberation
and peace, reconciliation and joy; the psalmist prays for
a ruler who will light the way of his people with righteousness, prosperity, and an end to oppression and injustice. The writer of Ephesians lights the way through
mystery, with a message of the good news of Christ Jesus; and the Magi follow the light of a star, finding more
than they were looking for to return home transformed.

Invitation and Gathering

Centering Words (Isa 60, Matt 2)

Light shines in the darkness. A star guides our way to
the Christ-child. Hope is born again.
(*B. J. Beu*)

Call to Worship (Isa 60, Matt 2)

Arise; shine, for your light has come!
We are called out of our darkness into light.
Lift up your eyes and look around.
We rejoice in the gift of light.
Come let us worship the God of light and joy and peace.
We come to kneel at the cradle of the babe,
the light incarnate.

–Or–

Call to Worship (Isa 60, Matt 2)

Light has broken in on the darkness of the world!
Can you see it? Can you feel it?
Open the eyes of your heart and light the light within.
There is a star beckoning us to follow.
Let's go and see where it leads us today in worship.
Let's see where it leads us tomorrow
as we go about our day, our week,
and the rest of our lives.

Opening Prayer (Isa 60, Ps 72, Matt 2)

God of promise and light,
open our eyes this morning,
that we may see your light in the darkness.

Open our hearts,
　　that we may perceive your promises
　　　　of justice and righteousness
　　　　　　fulfilled in the babe of Bethlehem.
May we, like the Magi,
　　have a star to guide us
　　　　on our journey quest
　　　　　　to find the one who will truly set us free.
May this time of worship
　　bring us closer to you,
　　　　that the good news
　　　　　　of the birth of light and love
　　　　　　　　will transform our lives. Amen.

Proclamation and Response

Prayer of Confession (Isa 60, Ps 72, Matt 2)
Ever patient God,
　　we are a people who live in thick darkness.
We stumble around,
　　bombarded by news of war and poverty,
　　　　famine and genocide,
　　　　　　injustice and oppression.
The maelstrom of things and issues
　　and people of the dark,
　　　　can overwhelm and paralyze us.
Help us to be people of the light,
　　shining your light of righteousness, peace, and joy
　　　　into all the dark places of our lives and world.
Unlock the mystery and glory
　　of the babe born in Bethlehem.

Turn our aimless wanderings
    into a journey of purpose
        guided by your star.
Let the light break into our lives and our world,
    and transform us into people of the light.

Words of Assurance (Isa 60, Matt 2)

As certain as the dawn follows the night,
    so is the promise of God's forgiveness
    and love for us all.
Arise and Shine.
Follow the star.
Find the light of the world born in Bethlehem...
    and be transformed from darkness into light.

Passing the Peace of Christ (Isa 60, Matt 2)

Lift your eyes and look around. The light of the babe of Bethlehem shines from the face of each one here. Let us now greet that light, rejoice that we are here together, and pass the peace of Christ, our joy and our hope.

Invitation to the Word (Isa 60)

Open our hearts and minds to the light of your word
    read and preached.

Response to the Word (Isa 60, Matt 2)

Arise and shine, for your light has come.
Lift up your eyes and look around.
Praise the God of promise and light and love.
Praise the God of the guiding star.

–Or–

Response to the Word (Isa 60, Matt 2)
>We rejoice in the mystery made plain
>>through the good news of the babe of Bethlehem.
>May this Good News transform us
>and guide us as we seek to follow the star
>of love and light.

Thanksgiving and Communion

Invitation to the Offering (Isa 60, Matt 2)
>We have seen the light of the world. We have been called to follow the star of promise. Like the Magi, let us bring our gifts to honor the babe of Bethlehem and bring the light to all the dark places in our community and our world.

Offering Prayer (Isa 60, Matt 2)
>God of light and promise, we bring our gifts
>>to further your work in a dark world.
>May they bring your light
>>to those overwhelmed by darkness, pain,
>>>and loneliness.
>Accept these gifts of money and time,
>>indeed, the gift of our very selves.
>Let them shine for all to see,
>>and be brought into the sphere of your love
>>>and righteousness.

Sending Forth

Benediction (Isa 60, Matt 2)
Arise, and go forth to shine for all the world to see.
**We go to spread the good news of light and love,
righteousness and justice.**
Go now and follow the star
that will guide you on your journey
this week, this year, and forever.
**As the Magi of old,
we go forth in trust and excitement,
transformed in the presence
of the child of light.**
May the blessing of the God of light
rest upon you and fill you with light.
Amen.

January 10, 2021

Baptism of the Lord

Mary Scifres

Color

White

Scripture Readings

Genesis 1:1-5; Psalm 29; Acts 19:1-7; Mark 1:4-11

Theme Ideas

The power of speech flows through each of today's readings. God speaks and creation begins. God's voice thunders over the waters, displaying God's glory. Paul speaks and people are convinced to receive baptism in the Spirit's power. And at Jesus's baptism, God speaks a blessing of love, and claims Jesus as God's own child. With our words and with God's word, creation begins, as does our own re-creation in baptism.

Invitation and Gathering

Centering Words (Gen 1, Mark 1)

Speaking words of love, God creates us, calls to us, and claims us as God's own. Speaking words of love, we too can create, call, and claim God's beauty and glory in the world.

Call to Worship *(Gen 1, Ps 29, Mark 1)*
God's strong voice calls us to worship,
    calling us to sing and offer praise.
God's creative voice calls us to worship,
    calling us to life and light.
God's loving voice calls us to worship,
    calling us to love and be loved.
Listen, for God's voice calls to us now.

Opening Prayer *(Gen 1, Acts 19, Mark 1)*
Word of God, speak,
    for your servants are listening.
(Pause for silent prayer.)
Spirit of creation and renewal,
    hover over our gathering this day,
        as you hovered over creation on that first day.
Enter into our hearts and our lives,
    as you did at the day of our baptism.
Descend on us like a dove,
    as you did on Jesus's day of baptism,
        that we may hear again
            your words of love and adoption.
Speak from the heavens into our minds,
    that we may perceive your words of guidance
        and wisdom.

Proclamation and Response

Prayer of Confession *(Acts 19, Mark 1)*
When our hearts are hard as stone,
    soften us with your grace.
When our lives are riddled with sin and pain,
    heal us with your mercy.

When our ears are ringing with self-doubt and cynicism,
strengthen us with words of faith and love.
When our minds are muddled with confusion and fear,
enlighten us with the radiance of your wisdom.
Speak to our spirits from the truth of your being,
the reality of your love,
and the promise of your forgiveness,
that we may hear your voice clearly
and follow where you call us to go.

Words of Assurance (Mark 1, Prov 8, Ps 16, Ps 147, Ps 149)
Hear the truth of God's voice
breaking through the clouds of our lives:
"You are my child, the one I dearly love.
I delight in your creation."
**"You are my child, the one I dearly love.
I delight in your creation."**

Passing the Peace of Christ (Mark 1)
Share together this blessing and truth:
**You are God's child,
beloved and pleasing to God.**

Introduction to the Word (Gen 1, Ps 29, Mark 1)
Listen, for as scripture is read, we may hear the voice of God thundering over the waters, hovering like a gentle breeze, or parting the clouds and speaking words of love. Listen, for God is speaking through the ages, and through ancient words, into a changing world with the unchanging promise of God's constant presence.

Response to the Word (Gen 1, Ps 29, Acts 19, Mark 1)
God has spoken,
and we have listened.

In ancient words of scripture,
in today's words of song and prayer,
in messages from long ago,
and in messages brought anew today.
God will keep speaking.
We will continue to listen.

Thanksgiving and Communion

Invitation to the Offering (Ps 29, Acts 19, Mark 1)
With hearts wide open and ears ready to hear, we bring
our very lives to this time of offering. May we bring more
than just gifts in a plate, but hearts and minds ready to
hear God's call and respond where God's voice leads us.

Offering Prayer (Gen 1, Acts 19, Mark 1)
Bless these gifts with your voice of creation,
your healing, and your love, Mighty God.
Transform our meager offerings into abundant gifts
for a world in need of your light and life. Amen.

Sending Forth

Benediction (Gen 1, Mark 1)
Amidst a noisy world, make way to listen for God.
In the busiest of days, find time to listen for God.
For in the listening, we finally hear this truth:
We are beloved children of God—
created in love, created for love, created to love.
Let's go out there to listen and love.

January 17, 2021

Second Sunday after the Epiphany
Mary Petrina Boyd

Color
Green

Scripture Readings
1 Samuel 3:1-10, (11-20); Psalm 139:1-6, 13-18;
1 Corinthians 6:12-20; John 1:43-51

Theme Ideas
God, who is beyond our comprehension, knows us intimately. God knew the boy Samuel before Samuel knew who God was. Jesus knew Nathanael before they met. Psalm 139 tells how God knows us completely. God knows us and calls us to the journey of faith, trusting us to follow.

Invitation and Gathering

Centering Words (1 Sam 3, Ps 139, John 1)
God knows us better than we know ourselves. God calls us, inviting us on a journey of love.

Call to Worship (1 Sam 3, John 1)
In the shadows of the night, God calls us.
Here I am, for you called me.

In the daylight, God calls us.
Here I am, for you called me.
God calls to each of us by name.
Here I am, for you called me.

–Or–

Call to Worship (John 1)
Who is calling us?
Come and see.
What might happen?
Come and see.
Jesus calls to us, "Follow me."
We follow the one who calls us.

Opening Prayer (Ps 139, 1 Cor 6)
Creating God, how deeply you know us.
In the mystery of your love,
you see who we are and who we might become.
Our bodies are your creation;
they are wonderfully made.
Our minds reflect your handiwork.
Our spirits are a gift from you.
You call us by name and invite us to follow.
Lead us now into the depths of your love. Amen.

Proclamation and Response

Prayer of Confession (1 Sam 3)
O God, you call to us.
We hear you,
but aren't sure who is calling.
We hear you,
but are distracted by many things.

We hear you,
    but are afraid to answer.
Open our hearts to your voice.
Help us set aside our doubts,
    our fears, and our distractions,
        that we may answer you faithfully. Amen.

Words of Assurance (Ps 139)
    God searches us, knows us, loves us, and forgives us.
    God's love shelters us and keeps us safe.

Passing the Peace of Christ (Ps 139)
    Each one of us is wonderfully made, the creation of
    God's love. As you greet one another, marvel at God's
    wondrous works!

Prayer of Preparation (1 Sam 3, Ps 139)
    We are here, O God, waiting to hear your word.
    Help us recognize your voice
        as we listen for your guidance.
    Search our hearts and open them to your call.
    We are ready for your word of love. Amen.

Response to the Word (Ps 139)
    Holy Mystery, we cannot count your thoughts,
        nor can we understand completely
            your plan for creation.
    You know us more intimately than we know ourselves.
    We flourish in the womb of your love.
    When you call us on new adventures,
        we turn to you with joy,
            amazed at your presence.
    Open our hearts to your invitation
        and give us the courage to follow. Amen.

Thanksgiving and Communion

Offering Prayer (Ps 139)
God, you are the source of all goodness and life.
We bring our offering to you this day,
knowing that all we have comes from you.
We hear your call and we answer,
bringing all that we have and all that we are.
Use our gifts, our talents, and our bodies
for your work of peace and justice. Amen.

Sending Forth

Benediction (Ps 139, John 1)
God, who knows us better than we know ourselves,
calls us to follow.
**We go in Jesus's name to share the good news
of God's love.**
Go in peace, knowing that God loves you.
**We follow the call of Love
and go with God's abundant blessing.**

January 24, 2021

Third Sunday after the Epiphany

B. J. Beu

Copyright © B. J. Beu

Color

Green

Scripture Readings

Jonah 3:1-5, 10; Psalm 62:5-12; 1 Corinthians 7:29-31;
Mark 1:14-20

Theme Ideas

A sense of urgency marks these readings—a feeling that
time is short, or is already at hand. Jonah prophesies to
the Ninevites that they will meet their doom at God's
hands in forty days' time. Paul counsels the church of
Corinth that time is short—indeed, the present form of
this world is already passing away. And Jesus proclaims
that the time is fulfilled, for the kingdom of God has
come near. Whether the time is near, at hand, or seem-
ingly over, faithful action is called for. If true faith and
repentance can save Nineveh, it can save us. With the
psalmist, we are called to put our faith and trust in God,
who is our rock and our salvation.

Invitation and Gathering

Centering Words (Ps 62)

God is our rock and our salvation, whom shall we fear?

Call to Worship (Ps 62)

For God alone our souls wait in silence.
In God alone do our spirits find peace.
For God alone is our rock and our salvation.
In God alone does our faith remain unshaken.
Pour out your hearts before God.
For God is our refuge and our strength.
Put your trust in God.
God's steadfast love endures forever.

–Or–

Call to Worship (Mark 1)

Did you hear the good news?
The kingdom of God has drawn near.
Do you trust the good news?
We place our trust in Jesus,
the one who calls us to follow him.
Do you have the courage
to leave your former lives behind?
We put our faith in the Lord,
our rock and our salvation.
Trust the Lord.
We will follow Jesus.

Opening Prayer (Ps 62, Mark 1)

Teach us anew, rock of our salvation,
how your kingdom has come near.

As you called Simon and Andrew long ago,
>   call us to be your disciples this day,
>> that we might find refuge and strength
>>> as we face the destructive forces of our lives.
Grant us the strength to wait for you in silence,
>   that we might meet you
>> in the subterranean chambers of our souls.
For in you we rest secure,
>   in you we abide in holy love. Amen.

Proclamation and Response

Prayer of Yearning (1 Cor 7, Mark 1:15 NRSV)

Mighty God, the words of your Son echo in our ears:
>   "The kingdom of God has come near;
>> repent, and believe in the good news."
How we long to set aside the advice of others
>   and put our trust firmly in you.
How we yearn for the faithfulness of James and John,
>   who immediately left their boats to follow Jesus.
We know our fearful hearts, O God.
We know how far we are from being able to trust
>   a complete stranger—
>> especially with our very lives.
We hope to one day have their devotion,
>   even as we cannot find the nerve
>> to leave familiar paths behind.
Renew us, Holy One,
>   and bless us with your steadfast love,
>> that we might truly live as people
>>> who have seen your kingdom draw near.
Amen.

Words of Assurance (Jonah 3, Ps 62)
Just as God forgave the people of Nineveh
when they repented and turned from their ways,
so God will forgive us also,
when we turn to walk in the paths of life.
Pour out your hearts before God,
our refuge and our strength.
Pour out your hearts and find peace.

Passing the Peace of Christ (Ps 62)
With the joy that comes from waiting silently for God,
let us share signs of holy peace this morning/day.

Invitation to the Word (Mark 1)
Let us hear the word of God
as those for whom the kingdom has drawn near.
Let us heed the word of God
as those for whom light has dawned.
Let us live the word of God
as those for whom the ways of God
are deeply lived.

Call to Silent Prayer (Ps 62)
For God alone our souls wait in silence,
for our souls are restless
until they find their rest in God.
Into this holy presence, known only in silence,
let us come before the Lord,
our rock and our salvation;
let us find shelter in the Lord,
our refuge and our strength.
Let us pray.

Thanksgiving and Communion

Offering Prayer (Ps 62, Mark 1)
> God of abundance, you teach us the dangers
> of setting our hearts on earthly riches.
> May these offerings be symbols
> of our faith in your bounty,
> and of our commitment to follow
> your call in our lives,
> wherever you may lead. Amen.

Sending Forth

Benediction (Ps 62, Mark 1)
> Go as kingdom people,
> for the realm of God has come near.
> **We go with God's blessings.**
> Go as God's people,
> for that is who we are.
> **We go in the refuge of our rock
> and our salvation.**
> Go as those who believe in the good news,
> for that is our daily bread.
> **We go to live as people of mercy and grace.**

January 31, 2021

Fourth Sunday after the Epiphany

Mary Scifres

Copyright © Mary Scifres

Color

Green

Scripture Readings

Deuteronomy 18:15-20; Psalm 111; 1 Corinthians 8:1-13;
Mark 1:21-28

Theme Ideas

Our interactions with one another and with God matter.
This theme flows through each of today's readings. The
people are afraid to hear God directly, so God will send
them a prophet to act as their intermediary. Paul warns
the Corinthians that our actions and habits, even when
innocent and without fault, can become faults if they
cause confusion that leads others to harm. In Mark's
Gospel, even an evil spirit can recognize Jesus and proclaim who Jesus is. But as he casts the demon out of the
victim's life, Jesus brings the divine presence front and
center to a crowd that is now both shaken and confused.

Our interactions matter—sometimes bringing help and hope, other times not so much. Often, we won't know their effect until long after; but in the "now," we can simply interact to the best of our ability, with Christ's healing spirit and God's loving presence at the center of each interaction.

Invitation and Gathering

Centering Words (1 Cor 8)

If someone loves God, they are known by God. Love God, and trust that you are known by God.

Call to Worship (Ps 111, 1 Cor 8)

Praise God, who loves us all.
> **Praise God, who is full of mercy and compassion.**

Praise God, who loves us well.
> **Praise God, who creates honesty and justice.**

Praise God, who invites us to love.
> **Praise God, who loves through us**
> **and our actions.**

Opening Prayer (Ps 111, 1 Cor 8)

Loving God, love through us,
> as we worship your holy name.

Love through us,
> as we listen for your holy word.

Love through us,
> as we live your teachings
> > and offer your love to our world.

In your majestic name, we pray. Amen.

Proclamation and Response

Prayer of Confession (1 Cor 8, Mark 1)
> When we cry out with words that hurt,
>> silence our cries
>>> and speak gently through our words.
> When we act in ways that hurt,
>> even when help is intended,
>>> transform our hurtful actions with your grace.
> When we forget that we are loved and called to love,
>> love us back into your likeness,
>>> that your love might flow freely through us
>>>> and bring your love to the world.
> In your holy presence of love, we pray. Amen.

Words of Assurance (Ps 111, 1 Cor 8)
> Full of mercy and compassion,
>> God knows us to the core of our being,
>> and loves us through all of our days.

Passing the Peace of Christ (1 Cor 8)
> Our acts of love and peace have the power to transform lives. In the powerful love of Christ, let us share signs of peace to transform this church and this world with love.

Introduction to the Word (Ps 111, Mark 1)
> Prepare to be amazed again at God's teachings,
>> for God's teachings are amazing still.
> Prepare to discover wisdom,
>> for God's word is full of wisdom and truth.

Response to the Word (1 Cor 8)
> Glorious God, even as we belong to you,
>> we are loved by you.

In this love, we are transformed into new creations
again and again.
With this love, we are given power and opportunity
to transform others with acts of love and grace.
Love through us, even as we are loved,
that your world may grow ever closer to you
and that we may grow ever closer
to your likeness. Amen.

Thanksgiving and Communion

Invitation to the Offering (1 Cor 8)
As actions of grace and love, let us offer our gifts and
lives to God.

Offering Prayer (Ps 111, 1 Cor 8)
Holy, awesome God, we bring gifts of paper and coin,
symbols of our gratitude and our love.
Bless these symbols,
that they may become acts of love and grace.
Bless us and our gifts,
that we may transform the world
with love and grace.
In gratitude and hope, we pray. Amen.

Sending Forth

Benediction (1 Cor 8)
Go now to love as beloved children of God.
Go now to live as living signs of Christ's presence.
Go now to transform the world
with the power of the Holy Spirit.

February 7, 2021

Fifth Sunday after the Epiphany

Laura Jaquith Bartlett

Color

Green

Scripture Readings

Isaiah 40:21-31; Psalm 147:1-11, 20c; 1 Corinthians 9:16-23;
Mark 1:29-39

Theme Ideas

Proclaiming the gospel is *not* optional, says Paul! That
seems like a no-brainer, but how many of us intention-
ally fill our days proclaiming the gospel? The gospel
message is chock-full of the good news of love—not just
any love, but the love of the everlasting God. This is the
one who created the earth and the heavens, who provides sustenance, strength, compassion, and healing for
all creatures, and who takes delight in those who place
their hope in the tenacious and tender power of divine
love. How can we keep quiet in the face of this amazing
truth?

Invitation and Gathering

Centering Words (Isa 40, Ps 147, 1 Cor 9, Mark 1)

(Suggestion: "How Can I Keep from Singing?" would be a good prelude or gathering song before worship begins.)

How can we keep silent if we truly know the awesome power, mercy, and love of God?

Call to Worship (Isa 40, Ps 147, 1 Cor 9)

Voice 1: Is anyone here feeling tired?

Voice 2: YES! I am weary and weighed down with burdens.

All: Take heart! God gives us strength and energy.

Voice 1: Is anyone here hurt or grieving?

Voice 2: YES! I am wounded and in pain.

All: Take heart! God heals broken hearts.

Voice 1: Is anyone here short on cash, pinched for resources?

Voice 2: YES! I am overwhelmed with debt and the effort of making ends meet.

All: Take heart! God's reward is free for the taking.

Voice 1: Is anyone here left out, shunned, outcast?

Voice 2: YES! I have been pushed to the margins, labeled unworthy of inclusion.

All: Take heart! God is calling your name and waiting to gather you close in love!

Opening Prayer (Isa 40, Ps 147, 1 Cor 9, Mark 1)

Holy One, with our ancestors and all the people of God, we gather to sing your praises.

You are the one who has created the cosmos
    and the ants.
You give food to whales and sparrows,
    name the stars, and count the hairs on our heads.
Compassionate One, we offer you our thanksgiving
    for your many blessings.
Powerful One, inspire us this day:
    to turn our praise into action,
    to share your good news
        with those who long to hear a word of hope,
to proclaim your message of peace and justice
    throughout the world.
Praise to you! Amen.

Proclamation and Response

Prayer of Confession (Isa 40, Ps 147, 1 Cor 9, Mark 1)
God of Strength, we confess our doubt.
    We are weary, but we turn to caffeine
        instead of waiting to be carried effortlessly
            on your eagle's wings.
    Forgive us, we pray.
(silence)
God of Justice, we confess our lack of trust.
    We are outraged and angry,
        but we turn to name-calling, tweeting,
            and demonizing others
        instead of waiting for you to lift us up
            from the pit.
    Forgive us, we pray.
(silence)

God of Grace, we confess our reticence.
> **We praise you with enthusiasm on Sunday,**
>> **but then we turn to safe clichés**
>>> **about separating religion and politics**
>> **when we could be proclaiming the message**
>>> **of your limitless love.**
>> **Forgive us, we pray.**

(silence)

Words of Assurance (Isa 40:31 NRSV, 1 Cor 9)

(The final silence is ended with instrumental music playing "On Eagle's Wings" [United Methodist Hymnal #143]; the music continues under the Words of Assurance.)
Hear God's promise to all:
> "Those who wait for the Lord
> shall renew their strength,
> they shall mount up with wings like eagles,
> they shall run and not be weary,
> they shall walk and not faint."

Know that God's promise of grace and forgiveness
> is free of charge!

(Respond to these words by singing the refrain of "On Eagle's Wings.")

Passing the Peace of Christ (Isa 40, 1 Cor 9)

Each one of us has come here today needing to hear words of peace, grace, and love. Spend the next minute offering these words with those around you: "God's love is for *you*." Respond by saying, "Hallelujah!"

Prayer of Preparation (Isa 40, Ps 147, 1 Cor 9, Mark 1)

You who formed us, named us, and gathered us,
> open our ears to hear your message.

You who give power to the faint,
    help us understand your message.
You who uplift, strengthen, and heal,
    inspire us to proclaim your message.
We pray in the name of Christ, who *is* the Message.
Amen.

Response to the Word (1 Cor 9, Mark 1)

It's time now for the [*insert the name of your own faith community*] Quiz Show! All you need to do is answer each question correctly. Let's see if you can do it!
When you leave today, what are you called to do?

Proclaim the Gospel message of God's love.
When you encounter people who are lonely,
what are you called to do?

Proclaim the Gospel message of God's love.
When you encounter people who are discouraged,
what are you called to do?

Proclaim the Gospel message of God's love.
When you encounter people who are hurting,
what are you called to do?

Proclaim the Gospel message of God's love.
When you encounter people who are different,
what are you called to do?

Proclaim the Gospel message of God's love.
When you encounter people who are marginalized,
what are you called to do?

Proclaim the Gospel message of God's love.
Every minute of every day,
what are you called to do?

Proclaim the Gospel message of God's love.
We are all big winners when we share the blessings
of God's love!

Thanksgiving and Communion

Offering Prayer (Isa 40, Ps 147, 1 Cor 9, Mark 1)
>God, you have created the universe.
>Everything we see has come into being because of you.
>Your glory is beyond our comprehension.
>Yet, you give us the most precious gift imaginable:
>>your everlasting love and faithfulness.
>With great joy we now offer our own gifts—
>>puny in comparison, but given with grateful hearts
>>>that belong to you, now and always.
>We are thankful for the opportunity
>>to put these gifts to work
>>>proclaiming your gospel of love. Amen.

Sending Forth

Benediction (Isa 40, Ps 147, Mark 1)
>The God who named the stars has named each of us.
>Remember that God is calling *your* name.
>>**We will answer God's call**
>>**to proclaim the gospel of love.**
>Jesus Christ healed, cast out the demons,
>and made people whole.
>Jesus offers *you* wholeness.
>>**Healed by Christ, even in our brokenness,**
>>**we go to proclaim the gospel of love.**
>The Holy Spirit anointed Mary, birthed the church,
>and is right now blowing you out this door!
>>**Empowered by the Spirit,**
>>**we go out to proclaim the gospel of love!**
>>**Amen!**

February 14, 2021

Transfiguration Sunday

Mary Scifres

Copyright © Mary Scifres

Color

White

Scripture Readings

2 Kings 2:1-12; Psalm 50:1-6; 2 Corinthians 4:3-6; Mark 9:2-9

Theme Ideas

Although God's presence shines brightly in today's mystical scriptures, the brightness of God's presence and message shines most clearly in our hearts and minds. The visible brightness of God is perhaps too much to take in, and so God speaks more gently through our hearts, our memories, and through the shadowy moments of life. Only after Elijah has disappeared can Elisha proclaim what he has seen; only after the clouds overshadow the disciples are they able to hear God's message. Paul reminds us that light shines out of darkness, and that our deepest knowledge comes from the light shining through our hearts. This is the transformative power of God's presence—not just surrounding us, but abiding within us.

Invitation and Gathering

Centering Words (2 Kgs 2, 2 Cor 4, Mark 9)
May the brightness of God shine around us, within us,
and through us.

Call to Worship (Ps 50, 2 Cor 4, Mark 9)
The light of God is shining...
shining around and within.
The voice of God is calling...
calling not just from ancient texts,
but from here and now.
The love of God is with us...
flowing around and within us.

Opening Prayer (2 Kgs 2, Mark 9)
Stay with us, Creator God.
Live in us, Christ Jesus.
Abide in us, Holy Spirit.
Amen.

Proclamation and Response

Prayer of Yearning (2 Kgs 2, Mark 9)
Shine upon us with your grace,
that we might see what frightens us
and face what threatens us.
Flow through us with your mercy,
that we might sense your presence,
even when we have run away,
and that we may know your love,
even when we feel most unlovable.
Abide in us with your love,
for your love claims us and makes us whole. Amen.

Words of Assurance (2 Cor 4)

Even in the darkest of times, the light of God is shining.
The light of Christ's love and mercy are shining now,
> brightening our lives with mercy and grace.

Passing the Peace of Christ (Mark 9)

Share signs of light and love, for in these signs we experience the peace of Christ—the mysterious peace that passes all understanding.

Introduction to the Word (Ps 50)

Listen, for God speaks, calling out to the earth,
> speaking for all to hear.

Response to the Word (2 Cor 4, Mark 9)

The light of God is shining.
The word of God is speaking.
In this time of silence,
> may we look within and listen deeply
> for the presence of God in our midst.

(Allow time for silent prayer or meditation. Conclude the time with a choral response, quiet congregational song, or simply say, "Amen.")

Thanksgiving and Communion

Invitation to the Offering (2 Cor 4, Mark 9)

In a world of shadows and clouds, we are invited to proclaim the light of Christ. As the ushers wait upon us, may light guide our thoughts and help us know how to give of ourselves and our gifts so that we may become lights in a shadowy world.

Offering Prayer (2 Kgs 2, Ps 50, 2 Cor 4, Mark 9)
 God of light and love,
   shine through the gifts we bring before you now.
 Speak through our hearts and our actions.
 Bless our gifts, our offerings, and our very lives,
   that we may bless others with your presence.
 Amen.

Sending Forth

Benediction (2 Cor 4, Mark 9)
 May the brightness of God light our way.
 May the brightness of Christ shine within us.
 May the brightness of God's Spirit flow through us.

February 17, 2021

Ash Wednesday
Bill Hoppe

Color

Purple

Scripture Readings

Joel 2:1-2, 12-17; Psalm 51:1-17; 2 Corinthians 5:20b–6:10; Matthew 6:1-6, 16-21

Theme Ideas

Ash Wednesday is the beginning of Lent, the transition from death to life; the transition from the darkness and despair of the Day of the Lord to the light and hope of the Day of Salvation at Easter. We confront our own frailties and imperfections as we examine ourselves in the mirror of these readings. We see the reflection of arrogant hypocrites and hopeless sinners against the light of the Lord, who is justified in passing judgment. On the verge of certain destruction, *even then*, God reaches out to us with both hands, calling us to return and be reconciled. We meet the Lord in that secret place deep within—and in this encounter, our spirits become whiter than snow. We forgive and are forgiven, and begin to understand the extent of God's relentless affection for all.

Invitation and Gathering

Centering Words (2 Cor 5)
> As Christ's ambassadors to the world, let us be reconciled with God.

Call to Worship (Joel 2, 2 Cor 5)
> A trumpet sounds from afar.
>> **Listen, God is calling.**
> What does the Lord say to us?
>> **Now is the time. Today is the day.**
> Now is the time to return to God.
>> **Today is the day of our salvation.**
> Our sins cover us like mist upon the mountains.
>> **But you, Lord, have shown us your forgiveness.**
> Praise our God of grace and constant compassion!
>> **Thanks be to our Lord!**

–Or–

Call to Worship (2 Cor 5–6)
> We implore you in Christ's name, and on his behalf:
> Be reconciled to God.
>> **The Lord's grace is freely given to us.**
> Don't let it be in vain.
>> **Though he was innocent,**
>> **he suffered for our sake.**
> Let us honor this gift by becoming one with God,
> and one with Christ's faithful disciples everywhere.

Proclamation and Response

Opening Prayer (Ps 51, Matt 6)
> Our hearts are laid bare before you, Lord.
> You see us as no one else does.

You see past the impostor's masks we wear.
O God, we come to worship you,
    not with empty words and hollow acts of piety,
        but with lonely, aching spirits.
We long for the days of joy and gladness
    we have known with you.
Fold back the darkness that surrounds us.
Show us your mercy.
Cover us with your grace.
We return our whole hearts to you this day,
    as we pray humbly together in Jesus's name. Amen.

Prayer of Confession (Ps 51)
Lord, you abound in grace and mercy.
    Wash away our guilt,
        and cleanse us from our sins.
There's no way to hide what we've done.
    Our misdeeds constantly confront us.
We deserve your judgment.
    But we plead for your forgiveness.
You alone can change us and transform us.
    You alone can restore our joy.
Create a pure heart within us, Lord.
    Renew us, revive us, and uphold us.
Open our mouths, that we might proclaim your praises.
    Give voice to your songs of deliverance. Amen.

Words of Assurance (Ps 51)
The Lord takes little pleasure in our earthly offerings,
    but delights in the sacrifice of our broken spirits.
God will never turn away a wounded heart.

Response to the Word (Ps 51, Matt 6)

We make a show of our faith and devotion
   on far too many occasions, Lord.
We pride ourselves in our eloquent yet insincere prayers,
   fooling ourselves that you give credence
      to such nonsense.
We forget that you already know our needs
   long before we begin to pray.
We store up treasures on earth,
   rather than in heaven.
O God, we earnestly seek your forgiveness.
Return us to your secret place
   of divine wisdom and holy mystery—
      the place where you are always ready to meet us,
      the inner chamber of our hearts—
         where we worship you in spirit and truth.
In the name of Jesus, we pray. Amen.

Invitation to Imposition of Ashes (Joel, 2 Cor 5–6, Matt 6)

Blow the trumpet in Zion and assemble the congregation as we tremble in anticipation. The day of the Lord is near! We come ready to listen, watch, and wait. We come prepared to cleanse our souls and purge our spirits of all impurities. The time is right and the time is now. May the ashes of our lives bring healing within, as we receive these ashes upon our foreheads. We ask for God's blessing, and God's ever present love and mercy, as we receive the sign of our willingness to walk with Christ all the way to the cross. Amen.

(Sara Lambert)

Thanksgiving and Communion

Offering Prayer (Joel 2, Ps 51, Matt 6)

All that we have comes from you, Creator and Sustainer.

May these symbols of your gifts

 bring light to a dark and treacherous world,

  just as your truth brings joy and gladness to all.

Receive our earthly treasure,

 given freely for your good work

  in humanity's name. Amen.

(Sara Lambert)

Invitation to Communion

We stand at your table, O Lord,

 to weep, fast, mourn, and pray.

The ashes of your grace

 mark us for your salvation.

In the breaking of the bread,

 and the pouring of the cup,

 we realize once again

 the awesome power of your love.

The sins of our past rinsed clean,

 we remember the sacrifice of your Son.

Let all come who are sincerely penitent

 and seek the love of God, through Christ the Son.

The table is open.

No obstacle stands in the way of those

 who truly search for truth and faith.

(Sara Lambert)

Sending Forth

Benediction (2 Cor 6)
Though we were overwhelmed by sorrow,
we can rejoice in Christ.
Though we were dead,
we are alive in Christ.
Though we had nothing,
we possess everything in Christ.
In Christ, the day of deliverance has dawned!
Amen!

February 21, 2021

First Sunday in Lent
Rebecca J. Kruger Gaudino

Color

Purple

Scripture Readings

Genesis 9:8-17; Psalm 25:1-10; 1 Peter 3:18-22;
Mark 1:9-15

Theme Ideas

In Mark's baptismal account, God erupts into the life
of Jesus. The heavens are "torn apart" (v. 1:10 NRSV),
and the Spirit descends with urgency and purpose on
this newly proclaimed Son of God. Whatever life has in-
volved before his baptism, Jesus leaves it behind when
he emerges from the Jordan's waters. He begins to speak
and live out the good news of God's powerful, reconfig-
uring presence in the world. But, in the arrest of John the
Baptist, and in the presence of Satan in the wilderness,
we see the threat that Jesus will face. Are we willing to
follow this beloved Son, to let God erupt into our lives,
to take the dare of a new life from God?

Invitation and Gathering

Centering Words (Ps 25, Mark 1)

I offer my life to you, God,
>   for I know that you love me dearly and faithfully.
I offer my life to you, God.
Teach me your paths.

Call to Worship (Ps 25, Mark 1:11 NRSV)

(Be sure your baptismal font is visible and, if moveable, in a central location. Out of sight, set up a microphone near a big bucket of water. As the liturgist reads "from the waters," have someone do some loud splashing that represents the movement of Jesus. Everything is in motion in this brief Marcan reading. Let the water help communicate this motion. An on-screen picture of the Jordan River or of a soaring dove will add to the worship experience.)

When Jesus was baptized in the Jordan River,
he emerged from the waters...
>   **to see the heavens splitting open**
>   **and the Spirit soaring down like a dove.**
When Jesus was baptized in the Jordan River,
he stood up from the waters and heard:
>   **"You are my Son, the Beloved;**
>   **with you I am well pleased."**
When Jesus was baptized in the Jordan River,
he emerged from the waters...
>   **to walk a new path**
>   **and to call the world to join him.**
Here comes God's kingdom.
Teach us your path, brother Jesus.
Now is the time!

Opening Prayer (Ps 25, Mark 1)
> Creator and Sovereign, our world and our lives
> > are often full of threat.
> We return to you in this place today
> > to be reminded that you do not abandon us
> > > to the hard realities of our lives.
> You are the one who saves us.
> You are the one who faithfully teaches us
> > your life-giving ways.
> You are the one who instills courage within us
> > to stand up from the waters of our baptism
> > > and to walk your path.
> Enter our hearts and lives for your powerful purposes,
> > in the name of our baptized brother Jesus
> > > and the soaring Spirit. Amen.

Proclamation and Response

Prayer of Confession (Ps 25, Mark 1)
> God of faithful love and powerful purpose,
> > there are times when we are open to your leading—
> > > times when we walk the path of Jesus
> > > > with courage and hope,
> > > > > even when doing so is fearful.
> At other times, we close ourselves off,
> > hoping that you won't tear open the skies
> > > and disrupt our lives completely.
> Following Jesus can be pretty risky.
> Your compassion and faithful love claim us forever,
> > as they claimed Jesus when he entered the Jordan
> > > and made a bold decision to follow you
> > > > on a new and uncertain path. Amen.

Words of Assurance (Ps 25, Mark 1)

Yes, God's compassion and love *are* forever!
What God said of Jesus at his baptism,
    God says to us today:
    You are my dearly loved children,
    whom I love deeply.
God forgives us and loves us dearly,
    now and forevermore.

Passing the Peace of Christ (Mark 1)

God calls Jesus "my Child," "my Son"—beautiful words
that get at their cherished relationship of oneness. God
is saying to Jesus, "We belong to one another!" Jesus
would later call all who follow him his brothers and
sisters. That means we belong to one another in Christ
Jesus. As cherished members of the family of God, let us
greet one another with the peace of Christ.

Prayer of Preparation (Ps 25, Mark 1)

Divine Teacher,
    teach us through the example of your life.
Bringer of Good News,
    call out your good news to us again.
Reign of God,
    break into our lives and our world right now.
Amen.

Response to the Word (Ps 25, Mark 1)

(Be sure everyone has a blank sheet of light blue paper.)
Each of you has a blank sheet of blue paper. Think of
this paper as the sky of some part of your life that God
may wish to split open in calling you to newness. What
part of your life is this? I invite you to write this on the
blue sheet. During our prayer, I will signal when to tear

this sheet as a sign that God is entering your life at this very point to transform it. Save these pieces. During the offering, you may place these torn pieces of paper in the offering plate as a sign of giving your life to God.
(Give some time for reflection.)

Brother Jesus, you arose from the waters of baptism
    to follow a new path.
God tore open the heavens above you
    and claimed you for a powerful purpose
        and a vital ministry.
    You call us now to change our hearts and lives
        for your kingdom.
What sky would you split open to call each of us—
    your beloved sons and daughters—
        to new paths?
    Tear open the heavens once again, O God.
(Hold your blue sheet high so everyone can see you tear it, and then spread your arms wide to invite all to tear their sheets.)
We offer our lives to you.
    Claim us and our lives
        for your powerful purposes,
            in the name of our baptized brother Jesus
                and the soaring Spirit. Amen.

Thanksgiving and Communion

Invitation to the Offering (Mark 1:15)
We can say with Jesus today, "Here comes God's kingdom!...Trust this good news!" Because we trust the power and love of God, and we live into God's kingdom, let us give the gifts of our lives to God, including

the pieces of our lives *(hold up the torn pieces of your blue sheet)* for God to transform. May our gifts announce God's inbreaking kingdom, transforming us and our world.

Offering Prayer (Ps 25, Mark 1)
Because you are the God who saves us,
 we give you these gifts.
Take our lives and our gifts
 and use them to save our world.
We put our hope in you. Amen.

Sending Forth

Benediction (Ps 25, Mark 1:15)
God continues to tear open the heavens of our world
and our lives, calling out with a voice of love:
 "You are my beloved children,
 whom I love deeply."
God continues to tear open the heavens of our world
and our lives, sending us onto new paths and missions.
 God changes our hearts and lives,
 and the Spirit pushes us in new directions.
"Now is the time! Here comes God's kingdom!"
 We are Jesus people.
 We are kingdom people.
 Now is the time! Amen.

February 28, 2021

Second Sunday in Lent

B. J. Beu
Copyright © B. J. Beu

Color

Purple

Scripture Readings

Genesis 17:1-7, 15-16; Psalm 22:23-31; Romans 4:13-25;
Mark 8:31-38

Theme Ideas

Naming, covenant, and faith focus today's scriptures.
With words of covenant and promise, God changes
Abram's name to Abraham, and Sarai's name to Sarah.
The psalmist declares God's name, beseeching the whole
world to come back to God in humble faithfulness. Paul
proclaims that God's promises to Abraham were due to
his faith and not the law. In Mark's Gospel, Jesus rep-
rimands Peter (the rock): "Get behind me, Satan"—for
Peter was putting human ways above God's. We have to
be humble and listen with discerning ears if we are to be
found faithful. In these scriptures, new names are sym-
bolic of new journeys, of proclamations of faith, and of

promises of covenantal relationship. These texts invite us to remain steadfast in faith during spiritual journeys with God, even as we are transformed by God's call and covenant.

Invitation and Gathering

Centering Words (Gen 17, Ps 22, Rom 4, Mark 8)
God's voice names us in holy love. Christ's voice chastens us when we go astray. The Spirit's voice draws us back to the paths of righteousness. Thanks be to God!

Call to Worship (Gen 17, Ps 22, Rom 4, Mark 8)
From generation to generation,
God names us and claims us.
Blessed be the Lord, our God.
When we try to tell God what to do, Christ chastens us
and leads us back onto the paths of life.
Let all who draw breath come back to the Lord.
From our earliest steps, the Spirit guides our steps
and sets before us the ways of life and death.
Let the faithful rejoice in the mysteries
of our God.
From generation to generation,
God names us and claims us.
Let heaven and earth praise God's holy name.

Opening Prayer (Gen 17, Mark 8)
Spirit of the ages, name us and claim us
according to your purposes,
as you once called Abram and Sarai
long ago.
Train our ears to hear your call,
and tune our hearts to open
at the sound of your voice.

As we pick up our cross to follow you,
>> raise us to newness of life.
For you call us to be children of your covenant,
>> heirs with your Son,
>>>> and disciples of your grace. Amen.

Proclamation and Response

Prayer of Yearning (Gen 17, Ps 22, Mark 8)
Name above all names,
>> visit us in our dreams
>>>> and shake us from our waking nightmares.
For we are tired of stumbling in the dark,
>> blindly following human teachings
>>>> and placidly heeding human advice.
When we lose our way
>> and wander from your path,
>>>> we need your love to heal us
>>>>>> and your grace to complete us.
When the forces of destruction close around us,
>> grant us the strength to follow Christ.
Love us back onto the right paths
>> and restore us to life,
>>>> through your faithful and transforming love.
Amen.

Words of Assurance (Mark 8)
By saying no to ourselves, and picking up our cross,
>> we find ourselves.
By saying yes to the good news of Christ's spirit,
>> we find faith and wholeness.
Thanks be to God.

Passing the Peace of Christ (Mark 8)

As followers of Christ, let us pick up our cross and follow him, even when the road is long. On this journey, let us draw strength from one another as we share signs of grace and peace.

Response to the Word (Gen 17, Mark 8)

In the midst of our everyday lives,
>you come to us with ancient truths, O God,
>>reminding us of who we are
>>>and whose we are.

You have called us and claimed us;
>we will not shut out the lessons you teach.

Renew your covenant with us this day,
>that our lives might shine
>>with the light of your covenant,
>and our souls might reflect
>>the light of your love.

Thanksgiving and Communion

Invitation to the Offering (Gen 17, Ps 22)

The psalmist proclaims that creation will remember and return to God. As those blessed to be a blessing to others, may we return to God with the gifts of our hands and hearts.

Offering Prayer (Gen 17, Ps 22)

God of manifold blessings,
>bless our lives to your service,
>>even as we consecrate these gifts
>>>in service of a world in need.

May our offering go forth this day,
    and be a reflection of your glory
        for all who struggle to know your ways.
As these gifts go forth to do your work,
    may they help others hear your voice
        as you call their names.
In the spirit of your grace and peace, we pray. Amen.

Sending Forth

Benediction (Gen 17, Rom 4, Mark 8)
Go forth with the voice of God calling your name.
    We go in the love of God.
Go forth to hear Christ claiming you as his own.
    We go in the mercy of Christ.
Go forth to follow where the Spirit sends you.
    We go in the power of the Holy Spirit.
Go forth, called, named, and claimed by God.

March 7, 2021

Third Sunday in Lent
Mary Scifres

Copyright © Mary Scifres

Color

Purple

Scripture Readings

Exodus 20:1-17; Psalm 19; 1 Corinthians 1:18-25;
John 2:13-22

Theme Ideas

The beauty and mystery of God's law flow through today's scriptures, even when that beauty and mystery
compel Jesus to create chaos in the temple as Passover
approaches. Paul proclaims the mysterious wisdom of
the cross, and our Hebrew scriptures proclaim the precious gift of God's commandments and teachings.

Invitation and Gathering

Centering Words (Ps 19, 1 Cor 1)

What if all our words were pleasing to God? Might we
discover wisdom and change the world?

Call to Worship (Ps 19, 1 Cor 1)
Called by Christ,
  we gather as one.
Blessed by God's wisdom,
  we gather to learn.
Amazed by God's love,
  we gather to worship.

Opening Prayer (Exod 20, Ps 19, 1 Cor 1, John 2)
God of glory and might,
  speak to us with your wisdom,
    that we might truly hear you.
Display your majesty,
  that we might truly see you.
Transform the chaos of our lives
  with the clarity of your call,
    that we might worship you in spirit
      and in truth. Amen.

Proclamation and Response

Prayer of Confession (1 Cor 1, John 2)
When we set up barriers that prevent others
  from knowing the truth of your love,
    forgive us and break down those walls.
When we set up barriers in our own minds and lives
  that keep us from knowing the truth of your love,
    break down our walls with your grace.
When we are confused by the world's wisdom,
  break through our muddled minds
    and shine the clarity of your teachings.
Draw us ever closer to you, to one another,
  and to the beauty of your wisdom and your love.
Amen.

Words of Assurance (Ps 19, John 2)
Christ reduces the barriers we set up to dust and ashes
that blow away to nothing in the power of his mercy
and his grace.
We are no longer divided or separated,
but are united in the wisdom and the love of God.

Passing the Peace of Christ (1 Cor 1, John 2)
We are one in God's wisdom. No barriers can separate
us from God or from one another. With joy, let us share
signs of our connection as we pass the peace of Christ.

Introduction to the Word (Ps 19)
God's wisdom is faithful; God's message is true. Let us
listen for the message of wisdom and truth this day.

Response to the Word (Ps 19, 1 Cor 1)
May the meditations of our hearts be pleasing
as we reflect on the words we have heard
and the message we have received.
May our lives be guided by God's wisdom and truth.
Amen.

Thanksgiving and Communion

Invitation to the Offering (1 Cor 1, John 2)
It is easy to offer our money and our gold, but God
desires our hearts and our lives. Even as we offer our
gifts in the offering plates this day, let us reflect on how
we might give our hearts and lives, so that others may
know the truth of God's wisdom and love.

Offering Prayer (1 Cor 1, John 2)
May the gifts we bring be gifts of love.
May the offerings we share be offerings of our hearts.

May each gift be blessed by your grace,
>   that others may know the truth of your wisdom
>   and your love. Amen.

Sending Forth

Benediction (Ps 19, 1 Cor 1)
Blessed by God's wisdom,
>   **we go forth refreshed and renewed.**
Called by Christ,
>   **we go now to serve.**
Amazed by God's love,
>   **we go now to love.**

March 14, 2021

Fourth Sunday in Lent

B. J. Beu
Copyright © B. J. Beu

Color

Purple

Scripture Readings

Numbers 21:4-9; Psalm 107:1-3, 17-22; Ephesians 2:1-10; John 3:14-21

Theme Ideas

As long as there have been people, people have acted badly. And as long as God has been with us, God has remained faithful. Numbers recounts the story of the Hebrew people grumbling against God and Moses in the desert, and how God saved the people from poisonous snakes. The psalmist rejoices in God's saving love—even for fools ensnared by their sinful ways. Ephesians proclaims that we were all like the dead because of our wrongdoing, but through Christ, we have been saved by the gift of God's immeasurable grace. Finally, John's Gospel proclaims that God sent the Human One into the world, not to condemn the world, but to save it. People keep messing up, yet God remains faithful.

Invitation and Gathering

Centering Words (Ps 107)
>Give thanks to the Lord, whose steadfast love endures forever. Let the faithful give thanks to the Lord.

Call to Worship (Ps 107, Eph 2)
>God is good.
>>**All the time.**
>
>And all the time,
>>**God is good.**
>
>Let all God's people cry out in joy:
>>**God's steadfast love endures forever.**
>
>Come! Let us worship the Lord of our salvation.

Opening Prayer (Eph 2, John 3)
>God of immeasurable grace,
>>you meet us in our time of need
>>>and cause your face to shine upon us.
>
>You sent your Son into the world,
>>that we might be saved;
>>>and you fashioned us into vessels
>>>>of your love and light.
>
>Redeem us this day, O God,
>>that we may be found worthy
>>>of the one who came to bring us life. Amen.

Proclamation and Response

Prayer of Yearning (Ps 107, Eph 2, John 3)
>Gracious God, we are tired of our own grumbling.
>Though we run around like errant children,
>>we long to return to your warm embrace.

Though we act as if the odds are stacked against us,
we yearn to rest in the knowledge
that your steadfast love endures forever.
Though we crouch in the shadows,
we long to feel the warmth of your love
shining upon us each day.
Lead us from death into life,
that we might live as children of light,
and serve one another as heirs of your Son,
in whose name we pray. Amen.

Words of Assurance (John 3)

God sent not his Son into the world to condemn it,
but that through him we might have eternal life.
The one who comes from above
saves us from our destructive ways,
and leads us into life.

Passing the Peace of Christ (Ps 107)

Thanking God for the bounty of love we find in Christ
Jesus, let us share our joy as we exchange signs of
Christ's peace this morning.

Response to the Word (Ps 107, Eph 2, John 3)

Through the immeasurable grace of God,
Christ leads us from death to life.
Through the gift of faith,
Christ brings us the gift of God's salvation.
By sending the Human One into the world,
God leads us from the shadows into the light.
Thanks be to God.

Thanksgiving and Communion

Invitation to the Offering (Ps 107, Eph 2)
From God's immeasurable grace, we have been saved by faith. In thankfulness for this mighty gift, let us give thanks to the Lord and offer God homage, as we offer back our tithes and our offerings.

Offering Prayer (John 3)
God of light and love,
as Jesus shined your light into our troubled world,
may our offering bring rays of your holy light
into the dark corners of our world.
May these gifts reach the places
where the fear of death holds sway,
that others may find Christ's life
in the midst of their pain. Amen.

Sending Forth

Benediction (Eph 2, John 3)
God sends us forth with the immeasurable gift of faith.
We will live in the joy of our salvation.
God sends us forth to walk in the light of holy love.
We will walk in the light of Christ.
God sends us forth in spirit and in truth.
We will journey in the Spirit's tender mercies.
Go with the blessings of God.

March 21, 2021

Fifth Sunday in Lent
Bob Rhodes

Color

Purple

Scripture Readings

Jeremiah 31:31-34; Psalm 51:1-12; Hebrews 5:5-10;
John 12:20-33

Theme Ideas

We are nearing the end of the season of Lent. A week
from now the traditional timing of Palm Sunday begins
followed by the Easter celebration of resurrection! This
is a time of anticipation, and this is reflected in the texts.
The prophet Jeremiah writes of the days that are coming, of a new covenant; the psalmist looks toward being
cleansed and restored; the letter to the Hebrews alludes
to our common aim of working toward perfection; and
the Gospel of John culminates our anticipation with the
reminder that the hour has come.

Invitation and Gathering

Centering Words (Jer 31)

We are changing. *You* are changing. God is already at work in you, renewing your spirit. Anticipate the new thing that God is doing. Can you feel it?

Call to Worship (Ps 51, John 12)

Have mercy on your people, O God.
> **Wash us. Cleanse us.**
> **Make us more perfect in your love.**

Open the skies and pour down your grace
upon your people.
> **Open our hearts to hear your voice.**
> **Let the thunder of your presence awaken us!**

Have mercy on your people, O God.
> **Restore within us the joy of your salvation.**
> **Draw us nearer to Jesus, our Christ!**

Opening Prayer (Ps 51, Heb 5)

God of love and mercy, open our hearts to your presence
as we worship you this day.
Whether our prayers are filled with celebration
or with loud cries and tears,
remind us that you are the source
of our eternal salvation.
Give us the strength
to respond faithfully to your transforming love,
that the joy of your salvation
might shine in and through us all.
Wipe away our wrongdoing,
clean our hearts, and make us more perfect.

For it is in your perfect love
>   that we are drawn more fully into your image.
In the name of the glorified Christ, we pray. Amen.

Proclamation and Response

Prayer of Confession (Ps 51)
>   God of steadfast love and mercy,
>   >   we have shielded our eyes
>   >   >   from the evil and injustice in the world.
>   We have turned away
>   >   from your forgiveness and your compassion,
>   >   >   and from your wisdom and your guidance.
>   We have allowed our voices to be silent.
>   Cleanse us.
>   Purify us.
>   Remind us that we still have much to learn,
>   >   and that you continue to teach us.
>   Fill us with your Holy Spirit,
>   >   that our faith in you might be renewed.
>   In humble confidence, we pray. Amen.

Words of Assurance (Heb 5, Ps 51)
>   In the grace of God, through the love of Jesus Christ,
>   >   and by the power of the Holy Spirit,
>   >   we are saved from brokenness and sin
>   >   and are restored to the joy of God's salvation.

Passing the Peace of Christ (Ps 51, John 12)
>   As people of faith, united in the steadfast love and
>   mercy of God, let us share the peace of Christ, who is
>   glorified for the sake of all.
>   **The peace of Christ be with you always.**

Response to the Word (John 12)
May we grow in anticipation of God's voice—
a voice that speaks to us still.
Let us hear and respond to the thunderous voice
that calls to us.

Thanksgiving and Communion

Invitation to the Offering (Ps 51, Jer 31)
As we anticipate the transformation already begun within us, as we look toward being made perfect in God's holy love, let us respond in the joy of our salvation and in the hope of God's covenant people.

Offering Prayer (Jer 31, John 12)
Generous and all-loving God,
grant us the wisdom to know you more completely.
Give us the hope to live as your people.
Inspire us to give of our spirits more fully,
in the faith that your promise is already within us.
As we give our gifts and tithes today,
we recommit ourselves to your service
and to the service of your people.
May we do so in response to your unending call
that beckons us and leads us home.
We pray as followers of the glorified Christ. Amen.

Sending Forth

Benediction (John 12, Ps 51)
In anticipation of the transforming love of God,
the salvation of Jesus Christ,
and the mercy of the ever-present Holy Spirit,
may you hear the thunderous voice of God
and be restored in the joy of your salvation.

March 28, 2021

Palm/Passion Sunday
Kirsten Linford

Color

Purple

Palm Sunday Readings

Mark 11:1-11; Psalm 118:1-2, 19-29

Passion Sunday Readings

Isaiah 50:4-9a; Psalm 31:9-16; Philippians 2:5-11;
Mark 14:1–15:47 or Mark 15:1-39, (40-47)

Theme Ideas

There are multiple ways to approach Palm Sunday—
from staying entirely with the triumphal entry into Jerusalem, to extending into the rest of Holy Week. Even
if other services are planned for Maundy Thursday and
Good Friday, it can be helpful to include a little fore-
shadowing of Christ's passion on Palm Sunday for any
who won't have a chance to worship again before Easter
morning. This service seeks to make room for both the
uplift of Palm Sunday and the struggle of the coming

passion. We will highlight themes of trust to tie the two together, as trust comes naturally in the midst of celebration but is harder to hold on to in the midst of pain. As Christ accompanies us to our hard places, let us accompany him now to his own.

Invitation and Gathering

Centering Words (Ps 118, Isa 50, Phil 2)
> O, give thanks to our God, whose goodness and mercy endure forever. Who answers our cries. Who sustains the weary with a word. Who takes human form to stand with us. Blessed is the one who comes in the name of the Lord. And blessed are we when we stand with him.

Call to Worship (Ps 118, Phil 2)
> O give thanks to our God, who is good.
> **God's steadfast love endures forever!**
> Blessed is the one who comes in the name of the Lord.
> **For Christ has opened the gates of righteousness,**
> **that we may enter.**
> He has emptied himself for love of us.
> **Christ took human form,**
> **that we might know we are known.**
> Holy One, you are our God,
> **and we give thanks to you.**
> We give thanks to our God, who is good.
> **God's steadfast love endures forever.**

Opening Prayer (Mark 11, Phil 2)
> Holy Brother, you have come in God's name
> and for our sake.

You have entered our souls
    in moments of shouted Hosannas
        and waving cloaks.
And you have come just the same
    to our late nights and our confused hearts.
Come to us again, Dear One,
    and let us follow you.
Let your name be on our tongues
    and in our hearts. Amen.

Proclamation and Response

Prayer of Confession (Ps 31, Phil 2)
    Mercy of Mercies, where you go
        we have often been afraid to follow.
    Sometimes the sorrows of our lives
        blind us to the pain in the lives of others.
    Even yours.
    When we are spent with sorrow,
        when our years are filled with sighing,
        when our souls waste away,
        when we can barely speak your name—
            we find it hard to trust your presence,
                though you have already made yourself
                    humbled and broken, just like us.
    Help us place our trust in you, no matter the cost.
    Our times are in your hands.
    Give us the courage and the strength
        to stay by your side. Amen.

Words of Assurance (Isa 50)
    God sustains the weary with a word,
        and so shall God sustain us.

The Holy One who helps us
  will not let us be put to shame.
Christ stands with us,
  bringing the grace of our longing.

Passing the Peace of Christ (Mark 11)
Let us greet one another as we would greet Christ, for
all come in the name of the Lord. Please turn and share
signs of Christ's peace.

Prayer of Preparation (Ps 19)
May the words of my mouth…
  and the meditations of our hearts
    be acceptable in your sight, O Lord,
      our strength and our redeemer. Amen.

Response to the Word (Phil 2)
God of Life, we give thanks
  that our strength is found in you.
May your word move within us and renew our faith.
May the same mind be in us that was in Jesus,
  that we might have courage enough
    to walk with him all the way to the cross.

Thanksgiving and Communion

Offering Prayer (Isa 50)
Gracious God,
  you have given us blessings beyond measure:
    hearts of mercy,
    hands of grace,
    and the presence of Christ
      in our souls and in our lives.

We can never repay what we have received,
    so help us carry it forward.
May we use the gifts of hearts and hands
    to sustain the weary
        in word and in deed.
May we be awakened to all who long for God's peace,
    and have courage enough to walk with them.

Sending Forth

Benediction (Ps 31)
    People of God, go together
        into this hard and holy week.
    Trust in God.
    Be filled with the Spirit.
    Walk with Christ to the end.
    For Christ's times are in our hands now,
        as ours have ever been in his.

April 1, 2021

Holy Thursday
Deborah Sokolove

Color

Purple

Scripture Readings

Exodus 12:1-4, (5-10), 11-14; Psalm 116:1-2, 12-19;
1 Corinthians 11:23-26; John 13:1-17, 31b-35

Theme Ideas

Just as God heard the voice of the Israelites as they were
oppressed under Pharaoh in Egypt, God continues to hear
the voices of all who suffer from any kind of bondage,
whether physical or spiritual. Jesus shows us what love
looks like as he washes our feet, offering us the sustaining
bread of life and the cup of healing. In Christ, we learn
how to serve one another in love, humility, and gratitude.

Invitation and Gathering

Centering Words (Ps 116)
On this day of remembrance, we lift the cup of salvation,
and give thanks to the Holy One for the bread of life.

Call to Worship (John 13)

Jesus calls us to the feast.

We come, ready to join his disciples
at the table of grace.

Jesus calls us to join him in love and service.

We come, ready to wash one another's feet.

Jesus shows us how to love one another.

We come, ready to worship the God who calls us.

Opening Prayer (Exod 12, Ps 116, 1 Cor 11, John 13)

God of Moses and Miriam,

God of those who followed Jesus

from Galilee to Jerusalem,

God of all who call on you today—

you delivered the Israelites from bondage in Egypt,

keeping them safe from harm,

as they ate the bread of affliction,

seasoned with salty tears and bitter herbs.

Today, you continue to hear the voices

of all who live in fear and pain,

offering them the bread of life

and the cup of salvation,

as a promise to deliver them

from despair and anguish.

As we remember the last meal

that Jesus shared with his disciples,

give us the courage to live as servants,

to love the world as you have loved us,

and to pour out our lives

as members of the body of Christ.

Amen.

APRIL 1, 2021

Proclamation and Response

Prayer of Confession (John 13)
Wellspring of Love, Source of Compassion,
Teacher of Truth,
you call us to wash the feet of others
as you have washed ours,
yet we are often unwilling
to kneel at the feet of our friends,
preferring to be served
rather than to serve.
You invite us to join all of creation at your feast,
yet we are unwilling to make room at our table
for someone we do not know.
You pour yourself out for the sake of the whole world,
yet we are often unwilling to let go
of our selfish desires.
Forgive us and free us from our unwillingness
to find our true life as the body of Christ—
a body given for the healing of the world. Amen.

Words of Assurance (John 13)
Hear the good news:
God washes our souls with love and grace
before we even ask.
In the name of Jesus Christ, you are forgiven.
In the name of Jesus Christ, you are forgiven.
Glory to God. Amen.

Passing the Peace of Christ (John 13)
Jesus taught us to love one another as his disciples, so
let us greet one another with signs of peace.
The peace of Christ be with you.
The peace of Christ be with you always.

Prayer of Preparation (Ps 116)

Source of Compassion, Teacher of Truth,
Wellspring of Love,
open our hearts and minds to your holy Word
as we listen to the words of scripture
and to the silences between them.
Amen.

Response to the Word (John 13)

Teacher of Truth, Wellspring of Love,
Source of Compassion,
as we live into the last hours
that Jesus spent with his disciples,
we give you thanks and praise.
For even though he was betrayed,
Christ is always in our midst
when we love one another.

Thanksgiving and Communion

Offering Prayer (1 Cor 11)

Holy Mystery, just as Jesus offered bread and wine
so that we might eat and drink,
we offer these gifts
to a world that is hungry for abundant life.

Great Thanksgiving

Christ be with you.
And also with you.
Lift up your hearts.
We lift them up to God.
Let us give our thanks to the Holy One.
It is right to give our thanks and praise.

It is a right, good, and a joyful thing
    always and everywhere to give our thanks to you,
    who saved the Israelites from slavery in Egypt
    and who continues to hear the voice of your people
    in times of trouble.
We give you thanks for the gifts of life and love,
    for your promise to feed us with your holy Word
    and to make us into members of the body of Christ.

And so, with your creatures on earth
and all the heavenly chorus,
we praise your name and join their unending hymn:
    Holy, holy, holy Lord, God of power and might,
        heaven and earth are full of your glory.
    Hosanna in the highest. Blessed is the one
        who comes in the name of the Lord.
    Hosanna in the highest.

Holy are you, and holy is your child, Jesus Christ,
    who walked among us from Galilee to Jerusalem
    and who continues to live in us today,
    showing us your face in the faces of those
    whose feet we wash
    and in your power of love to heal all things.

On the night in which he gave himself up,
    Jesus took bread, broke it, saying:
    "Take, eat, all of you.
    This is my body, broken for you.
    Whenever you eat it,
    do so in remembrance of me."
After supper, he took the cup, saying:
    "This is the cup of the new covenant,
    poured out for the healing of the world.

Whenever you drink it,
do so in remembrance of me."

And so, in remembrance of your mighty acts
in Jesus Christ, we proclaim the mystery of faith.
Christ has died.
Christ is risen.
Christ will come again.
Pour out your Holy Spirit on us,
and on these gifts of bread and wine.
Make them be for us the body and blood of Christ,
that we may be the body of Christ
to a world that is aching
and yearning to be made whole.
Teacher of Truth, Wellspring of Love,
Source of Compassion,
we praise your healing, gracious name.
Amen.

Sending Forth

Benediction
With Moses and Miriam and all the disciples,
let us go forth to kneel at the feet
of all who cry out for help,
offering our love and service
in the name of Jesus, who is the Christ.
Amen.

April 2, 2021

Good Friday

Karen Clark Ristine

Color

Black or none

Scripture Readings

Isaiah 52:13–53:12; Psalm 22; Hebrews 10:16-25;
John 18:1–19:42

Theme Ideas

Good Friday is the most cross-centric day of worship in
the Christian tradition. While the crucifixion of Christ
was an unconscionably violent act, Christ remained the
Prince of Peace to his very last breath. This is a day to
visit the cross with reverence and gratitude and awe. Yet
we know resurrection and new life are coming. Sunday
is coming. Easter is coming. Steep your worship in this
sacred story, yet help all remember that hope is nigh.

Invitation and Gathering

Centering Words (John 18–19)
We enter with reverence into the presence of the cross
at this memorial of the crucifixion. We remember this

loving act of Christ. We enter this sacred story. We open ourselves to Divine Love and the Holy Spirit here at the foot of the cross of Christ.

Call to Worship (John 18–19)

Draw near to the cross of Christ.
> **We draw near in awe and gratitude.**

Enter this ancient and sacred story.
> **We enter, open to transformation.**

Find your place in this holy narrative.
> **We seek to receive anew the grace and love of Christ Jesus.**

Opening Prayer (John 18–19)

Holy One, Author of New Life,
> open our hearts, minds, and souls
> > to enter again into this sacred journey
> > > of Christ's passion and death.

Help us walk in the way of Jesus.
Help us find our place on this path.
Invite our hearts to be moved
> and our faith to be stirred.

In your holy name, we pray.

Proclamation and Response

Prayer of Confession (Heb 10:22 NRSV)

Gracious Creator, we come into your presence,
> aware that our actions and our inaction,
> > our words and our failure to speak,
> > > have hurt your heart
> > > > and hurt the hearts of others.

We seek your grace and forgiveness.

We seek to be our best selves.
As scripture says: "Let us approach with a true heart
in full assurance of faith,
with our hearts sprinkled clean
from an evil conscience
and our bodies washed with pure water."
In gratitude for this cleansing grace
granted to us through Christ Jesus, we pray. Amen.

Words of Assurance (Heb 10)
Let us hold fast to the confession of our hope.
In the name of Jesus Christ you are forgiven.
In the name of Jesus Christ, you are forgiven.

Prayer of Preparation (John 18–19)
Lord of All Hopefulness,
as we hear the retelling of the journey of Christ—
from a garden that had been a place of prayer,
through trials and mockery and brutal death,
to a garden where his body was laid to rest—
harden not our hearts.
Give us the courage to lay bare our own vulnerabilities,
that we may see the sacred intersection of our lives
and the passion of Christ.
Even as we remember this day of crucifixion,
help us hold on to the hope
that resurrection and new life are near. Amen.
(Resource Note: The United Methodist Book of Worship *contains a Tenebrae Service [#355] that includes the John passion passage translated with a sensitivity to the Jewish origins of Christianity and without implying blame. See https:// www.umcdiscipleship.org/resources/a-service-of-tenebrae.)*

(In many congregations, the Good Friday service ends in silence after the passion story is read, with instruction to leave pondering the movement of Spirit in our lives. Use the following worship elements only as they may be needed in your context.)

Response to the Word (Ps 22:19 NRSV, John 18–19)
"O LORD, do not be far away!
O my help, come quickly to my aid!"
Do not be gone long, Lord Jesus.
We mourn this day, and we await the joy
that will come with the dawn of Easter morning.

Thanksgiving and Communion

Offering Prayer (Heb 10)
Creator of us all, on this day when we mourn
the cruelest acts of humanity,
we pray that you would infuse our lives
with the essence of the goodness of Christ.
Help us inspire one another to acts of love
and deeds of mercy and grace.
Receive these gifts of our hands
and the offering of our very lives,
that we may embody the presence of Christ
as we love and serve you.
We pray in faith, even with a courage we do not feel.
Call us to carry on in Jesus's name. Amen.

Sending Forth

Benediction

In hope, go out in the name of the one who created you.
In peace, go out in the way of Jesus.
In love, go out in healing presence of God's Holy Spirit.
Amen.

April 4, 2021

Easter Sunday
Mary Petrina Boyd

Color

White

Scripture Readings

Acts 10:34-43; Psalm 118:1-2, 14-24; 1 Corinthians 15:1-11; John 20:1-18 or Mark 16:1-8

Theme Ideas

At Easter, God called forth a radically new life, over-turning the power of death, and proclaiming the triumph of love. This is deeper than spring flowers and baby chicks. This is the in-breaking of God's affirmation that love is stronger than death, and that life will triumph over the powers of empire. There is mystery here. No one sees the moment of resurrection, yet we experience the results of that moment. We trust that God alone can transform the moment of despair into a life of joy.

Invitation and Gathering

Centering Words (John 20)

As we turn away from the tomb, we encounter the risen Jesus. As we look in wonder, Jesus calls us by name. Life, not death, is the deepest truth—God's word for all creation.

Call to Worship (John 20)

Christ is risen!
Alleluia!
The tomb is empty!
Alleluia!
Christ is alive!
Alleluia!

–Or–

Call to Worship (Ps 118, John 20)

This is the day that the Lord has made.
Let us rejoice and be glad in it.
This is the day that sees Christ rise.
Let us rejoice and be glad in it.
This is the day of new beginnings,
for Christ is risen.
Christ is risen indeed! Alleluia!

–Or–

Call to Worship (Ps 118)

Give thanks to the Lord, for God is good.
God's steadfast love lasts forever.
Enter the gates of righteousness.
Come before God with song.

We are alive today, praising God.
God is our strength.
This is the day the Lord has made.
Let us rejoice and be glad in it.

Opening Prayer (John 20)
God of hope, in the midst of death,
     you call forth life.
When all hope seemed gone,
     you raised Jesus from the grave.
We come before you today,
     longing for your life-giving presence.
God of new life,
     raise us up with all your people.
Lift us from the tombs of our despair and doubt,
     that we may rejoice in your power over death.
God of joy, fill our hearts with alleluias
     as we sing your praises.
Glory to God. Amen!

Proclamation and Response

Prayer of Confession (John 20)
God of life and love, like Peter,
     we gaze into the empty tomb and see only death.
Like Mary, we stand weeping over loss.
We so often feel hopeless.
We don't recognize any possibility for joy.
Surprise us with your work in the world.
May we dry our tears,
     as we dance into new life. Amen.

Words of Assurance (Ps 118)

God's steadfast love endures forever,
>   calling forth new life and joy.

–Or–

Words of Assurance (Acts 10)

The risen Jesus offers forgiveness of sins
>   through his name.
Rejoice, Jesus gives you new life.

–Or–

Words of Assurance (Ps 118)

The stone that the builders rejected
>   has become the chief cornerstone.
God uses all things to build God's realm of peace.

Passing the Peace of Christ (Acts 10)

In the life, death, and resurrection of Jesus, God brought peace to all creation. Share this joyous peace with one another.

Prayer of Preparation (Acts 10, John 20)

God of grace,
>   we come today to hear the story of Easter.
Open our hearts,
>   that we might hear your truth anew.
Be with us on the journey that leads to life and hope.
Amen.

Response to the Word (John 20)

The shadows of night gave way to the dawn of a new day. Instead of death, we find new life, new hope, and new possibilities. The one who knows us better than we know ourselves calls us by name. We have seen Jesus and have heard the good news of Easter.

Thanksgiving and Communion

Offering Prayer (John 20, 1 Cor 15)
> Living God, you give us the greatest gift of all,
> > the gift of new life.
>
> Grateful for this gift, we bring our offerings,
> > the work of our hands.
>
> Use our gifts to share your word of hope,
> > your promise of forgiveness,
> > > and your blessings with all creation.
>
> Grateful for your love, we offer ourselves,
> > that we might walk with our neighbors
> > > into your garden of love. Amen.

Sending Forth

Benediction (John 20)
> Christ is risen!
> > **Alleluia!**
>
> The tomb is empty.
> > **Alleluia!**
>
> Go with joy to meet the risen Christ.
> > **Alleluia! Amen!**

–Or–

Benediction (John 20)
> May God's blessing of new life be yours.
> May God's gift of peace fill your hearts.
> May God's promise of forgiveness give you hope.
> May you go forth to tell the good news:
> > We have seen the risen Lord! Alleluia!

April 11, 2021

Second Sunday of Easter

Mary Scifres

Color

White

Scripture Readings

Acts 4:32-35; Psalm 133; 1 John 1:1–2:2; John 20:19-31

Theme Ideas

There is power in the gathered fellowship of believers. The earliest believers trusted this power so completely that they shared everything in common. Perhaps they remembered the story of Thomas missing that Easter evening resurrection appearance because he was absent from the fellowship of disciples. Yet when they were again gathered together, Jesus came into their midst— and Thomas found faith abundant. The psalmist speaks of the blessing of unity in the gathered fellowship as precious anointing oil and as nourishing dew from Mount Hermon. And John's letter reminds us that our true fellowship is a fellowship not just of the gathered children of light, but the Father of light, who is Christ Jesus. We discover such power when we live in unity with Christ in our very midst, bonding us together and lighting our journey of faith.

Invitation and Gathering

Centering Words (Acts 4, Ps 133)
How beautiful when we live together in unity and love!

Call to Worship (1 John 1, Ps 133)
Come, walk in the light.
We walk together as children of light and love.
Come, gather in the love of God.
We gather together as children of light and love.
Come, live in the unity of God's Holy Spirit.
We live together as children of light and love.

Opening Prayer (Ps 133, 1 John 1, John 20)
Light of the world, shine upon us with your Holy Spirit.
Gather in our midst,
that we might know you are truly here.
Guide us in unity and love,
that we might be a blessing of unity and love
for the world.

Proclamation and Response

Prayer of Confession (Ps 133, 1 John 1, John 20)
You know us so very well, Christ Jesus.
You know our doubts and our questions,
and you love us enough to welcome such doubts
and questions.

You know our fractures and divisions,
    and you love us enough to invite us
        to forgive one another and live in unity.
You know the shadows that tempt us,
    and still you shine your light within,
        inviting warmth and welcoming us back
          to your path of peace and love.
Thank you for loving us
    and for inviting us on the journey of love.
Help us embrace this journey,
    that we may walk in the light,
        and live in unity together.
In your gracious love, we pray. Amen.

Words of Assurance (1 John 1, 1 John 2)
God is faithful in love and grace,
    making our confession welcome
    and cleansing for the soul.
Rejoice! We are children of light.
Even when we falter,
    God's love is strong enough to bring us back
    to the light of forgiveness and grace.

Passing the Peace of Christ or Call to Worship (John 20)
Peace be with you.
    And also with you.
Peace be in our midst.
    Peace be in our very souls.
Peace be the light on our path.
    Peace be the way of our world.
Peace be with you.
    And also with you.

Prayer of Preparation (Acts 4, Ps 133, 1 John 1, John 20)
God of light and love,
> open our hearts to your message of unity.

Open our minds to the light of your wisdom.
Open our lives to the call of your Spirit.
Reveal to us your holy presence,
> as we listen and learn this day.

In the name of Christ, we pray. Amen.

Response to the Word (Acts 4, Ps 133)
Look around. Everyone here is a brother or sister to you.
Everyone here is a part of this fellowship.
Everyone here has a gift to give.
Everyone here has a need to be met.
Look around. What might you give?
What might you ask for?
With whom might you share a bit of light and love?
Let us reflect and pray silently,
> as we look at one another
> and as we recognize that we are one family of God,
> one fellowship of love in Christ Jesus.

(Time of silence may follow.)

Thanksgiving and Communion

Invitation to the Offering (Acts 4:32)
Acts 4 tells us, "The community of believers was one in heart and mind. None of them would say, 'This is mine!' about any of their possessions, but held everything in common." Can you imagine the unity of spirit of those first believers? Can you fathom the power that the Spirit was able to impart to and through them? We are this same community of believers, invited to be of one heart

and mind and to share all that we have and all that we are. As the ushers wait upon us to receive this morning's offering, let's think about what it might mean to give of ourselves so fully that the Spirit could do anything and everything through us.

Offering Prayer (Acts 4)

Generous God, we offer you our gifts as best we can.
Although we don't share everything in common,
    as those first believers did,
        we are sharing these gifts,
            that they may be used for the common good.
Bless these gifts with the power of your Holy Spirit.
Bless us with a spirit of unity and love.
And bless our ministries,
    that we may bring your message of unity and love
        for all the world to know.
In your Holy Spirit, we pray. Amen.

Sending Forth

Benediction (Acts 4, Ps 133, 1 John 1, John 20)

Live in the light,
    the light of unity and love.
Live in the light,
    the light of faith and hope.
Live in the light,
    the light of God for all the world to know.

April 18, 2021

Third Sunday of Easter
James Dollins

Color

White

Scripture Readings

Acts 3:12-19; Psalm 4; 1 John 3:1-7; Luke 24:36b-48

Theme Ideas

This week's scriptures teach us how to discover the risen Christ in our midst. We gather, study scripture, and even interpret prophecy in new ways, seeing how a suffering servant could, in fact, be the true messiah. In Luke, Jesus offers the Bible study teaching this lesson. In Acts, Peter does the same to explain the healing of a man who was lame. First John and Psalm 4 counsel us to wait patiently, abiding with each other, even when we are disturbed or are struggling to recognize Christ's hope. May this Easter season grant us an increasingly clear view of Christ's saving work in the world today.

Invitation and Gathering

Centering Words (Luke 24, 1 John 3)
> For all who lose sight of hope, adjust our perspective,
> catch our eye, and touch us, Risen Savior, with your sur-
> prising presence.

Call to Worship (Ps 4)
> Answer us when we call, O God.
> Be gracious to us and hear our prayer.
> > **When we are in distress, you make space for us.**
> > **You put gladness in our hearts,**
> > **as with a fine feast.**
> When we are disturbed, may we not sin,
> but ponder things on our beds, and be silent.
> > **I will both lie down and sleep in peace.**
> > **For you alone, O Lord, make me lie down**
> > **in safety.**

Opening Prayer or Prayer of Confession (Luke 24, 1 John 3)
> Holy God, we give thanks that you often reveal yourself
> > to be different from our expectations.
> When we long for the love we have known in the past,
> > our eyes are dimmed to the beauty you reveal
> > > to us now.
> As your first followers struggled
> > to see how a suffering savior could be the messiah,
> > > we strain to recognize you still today.
> Come, Spirit, make yourself known
> > in the study of scripture,
> > in our songs of praise,
> > > and especially in the grace and love
> > > > we offer one another,

Make yourself known in every friend
 we have yet to meet in your good
  and blessed name. Amen.

Proclamation and Response

Prayer of Confession (Luke 24, Acts 3, 1 John 3)
Spirit of the Risen Savior,
 when we fail to recognize you,
  we become reluctant to follow in your way.
Just as the disciples struggled to comprehend
 how the Christ could have been a suffering servant,
  we find it difficult to see you
   in those who suffer today.
We resist starting down the path you have shown us
 until we know exactly where it will lead.
Free us from cynicism and fear.
Liberate your world from suspicion and prejudice.
Forgive us, Living Lord,
 and lead us wherever you will.

Words of Assurance (Luke 24, Rom 5)
Christ lived, died, and rose again for us,
 even while we were sinners.
This is proof of God's love for us.
In the name of Christ, we are forgiven!

Response to the Word (Luke 24, Ps 4, 1 John 3)
Spend time, here and now, with the risen Lord.
 We will see Christ when we sing together,
 when we study the scriptures,
 and when we serve a stranger in need.

Even when our vision grows cloudy,
we can remain with Christ amidst suffering and loss.
>**Let us remain with God's Spirit,**
>**until the clouds pass and our anger subsides.**
In Christ, God did not stay far off, but dwelt with us,
until we truly saw God's love.
>**Let us remain with one another,**
>**and with all of God's children,**
>**until Christ unmistakably appears.**

Thanksgiving and Communion

Offering Prayer (Adapted from Christ Has No Body, Teresa of Avila, 1515–1582)
>God of love, help us remember
>>that Christ has no body now on earth but ours,
>>>no hands but ours, no feet but ours.
>Ours are the eyes to see the needs of the world.
>Ours are the hands to bless the people we meet.
>Ours are the feet to do good in Christ's name.
>Bless, O God, the work of our hands
>>and these offerings,
>>>that they may be Christ's work in the world.
>Amen.

–Or–

Offering Prayer (Luke 24, 1 John 3)
>Generous God, you put love into human form in Jesus,
>>who lived, died, and was raised to eternal life.
>Receive now these offerings,
>>that your grace may live today
>>>through the work of your church.

We offer these gifts with our time,
 our commitment, and our love,
  that the world may witness, without doubt,
   that Christ is alive today.
In your holy name, we pray. Amen.

Sending Forth

Benediction (Luke 24, 1 John 3)
 Christ is alive and has met us here.
 Now let us meet God's Spirit among friends, strangers,
  and in all of creation.
 For God's love lives today and forevermore. Amen.

April 25, 2021

Fourth Sunday of Easter
Mary Scifres
Copyright © Mary Scifres

Color

White

Scripture Readings

Acts 4:5-12; Psalm 23; 1 John 3:16-24; John 10:11-18

Theme Ideas

Loving in truth and action transforms lives. Today's readings call us to love in truth and action, even when that call entails risk and sacrifice. Just as a shepherd cares and protects the sheep, we are invited to care and protect one another and those we serve. When we answer Christ's call to love in this way, we reflect the sacrificial love that God has shown us through Jesus's death and resurrection.

Invitation and Gathering

Centering Words (Acts 4, 1 John 3)
When we love with our lives, we become reflections of God for all to see.

Call to Worship or Response to the Word (Acts 4, 1 John 3)
Love one another, even when love involves risk.
We love as God loves us.
Love and care for others, even when caring is hard.
We love and care as God loves and cares for us.
Love in truth and action.
By this we are known as children of God.

Opening Prayer or Response to the Word (Ps 23, 1 John 3, John 10)
Shepherd of love, guide our thoughts and our actions,
that we too might become shepherds of love.
Speak to our hearts as we listen this day,
that our hearts may expand and embrace
all of your sheep.
Love us fully,
that we might love all of the flocks of your world
as fully as we are loved by you.
In your shepherding love, we pray. Amen.

Proclamation and Response

Prayer of Yearning (Ps 23, 1 John 3)
Merciful shepherd, give us the grace to love as you love.
Give us the courage to protect and care for others,
even when we are afraid.
Grant us the strength to love in truth and action,
even when loving this way challenges us.
Awaken our curiosity and empathy,
even when we tend to neglect the needs of others.
Forgive us when our love is absent,
and show us how to offer our love
with more than just words.

Shepherd us in our loving and in our living,
    that others may see in us
        the fruit of your goodness and mercy.
In your love and grace, we pray. Amen.

–Or–

Prayer of Yearning (1 John 3, John 10)

Merciful shepherd, give us the grace to love as you love.
Give us the courage to love people who frighten us.
Grant us the mercy to love with the same great love
    you have for us.
Guide us as we learn to hear and welcome
    different voices.
Love through us,
    that we may welcome and include every person
        to your community of love.
Awaken our hearts to your generosity,
    when we neglect to embrace and include others.
Forgive us when our love is absent,
    and renew your love in our hearts,
        that our love may expand and enfold
            all of your people on earth.
In your love and grace, we pray. Amen.

Words of Assurance (1 John 3)

The Spirit abides in each of us—
    loving us, loving through us, forgiving us,
    and forgiving through us.
We are loved and forgiven,
    even as we love and forgive.
Thanks be to God!

Passing the Peace of Christ (1 John 3)

Let us love, not just with words, but with our lives. In this spirit of love, let us share signs of peace and hugs of grace with one another.

Response to the Word (Acts 4, 1 John 3, John 10)

If we commit to loving in truth and action,
    how might our lives look differently
    in the week ahead?
(Time for silent reflection can follow.)
When we love in truth and action,
    we show Christ's love to the world.
Christ the Good Shepherd can love through us
    when we love with our deeds and with our lives.

Thanksgiving and Communion

Offering Prayer (1 John 3, John 10)

Shepherd of love, bless these gifts
    with the power and presence of your love.
May your love bring healing
    to a world in need of your touch.
May your grace bring hope
    to a world in need of your promise.
And may our love be a sign, for all to see,
    that you, who are love,
        are present in the world today. Amen.

Sending Forth

Benediction (Acts 4, 1 John 3)

Go now to love, even when love involves risk.

We go now to love, as God loves us.

Go now to care, even when caring is hard.

We go now to care, as God cares for us.

Go now to love, in truth and in action.

By this we are known as children of God.

May 2, 2021

Fifth Sunday of Easter

B. J. Beu

Color

White

Scripture Readings

Acts 8:26-40; Psalm 22:25-31; 1 John 4:7-21; John 15:1-8

Theme Ideas

God is love. Those who abide in love, abide in God.
And those who abide in Christ's love, abide in Christ.
For Christ is the vine, and we are the branches. By abiding in the vine, we bear the fruit of love. Apart from
the vine, we can do nothing. In Acts, Philip meets an
Ethiopian eunuch, teaches him the meaning of Isaiah's
suffering servant song, and helps him abide in the vine.
The psalmist speaks of the servant who leads the people to abide in God. John writes that true love casts out
fear and offers us Jesus's commandment to love one another. Truly, God is love. Those who abide in love, abide
in God.

Invitation and Gathering

Centering Words (1 John 4, John 15)

Christ is the vine. We are the branches. Abide in the vine, and you will abide in love.

Call to Worship (1 John 4, John 15)

Come to Christ, the true vine,
and bear much fruit.
We have come to abide in the vine,
and to bear the fruit of salvation.
Come to love one another,
for love is of God.
We have come to the household of love,
for God is love.
Come to set aside your fears,
for perfect love drives out fear.
We have come to love one another,
as God has loved us.
Come! All are welcome here.

Opening Prayer (John 15)

Divine Vinegrower, the soil of your love
nurtures the roots of our lives
each and every day.
As we consecrate ourselves into your loving care,
plant us in the soil of your love,
that we may abide in Christ, our true vine,
and bear the fruit of your love and grace.
Give us rain in seasons of doubt
and nourish our growth,
that our harvest of love may bless the world.
In your bountiful name, we pray. Amen.

Proclamation and Response

Prayer of Yearning (1 John 4, John 15)
Source of love and life, your glory knows no bounds.
We yearn to set aside our fears,
    but we are often afraid.
We long to love our sisters and brothers,
    but we often feel alienated from them.
We desire to abide in you as you abide in us,
    but we can't seem to figure out how.
Show us once more how to love,
    for only love can cast out our fear.
Show us how to love one another well,
    for only then can we truly know you.
Show how to abide in your vine,
    for only then can we bear the fruit
        that glorifies your name. Amen.

Words of Assurance (John 15)
When we abide in Christ, we abide in the vine
    of love and grace.
Abide in the vine, and receive mercy beyond measure.

Passing the Peace of Christ (Ps 107)
As we abide in Christ, our vine, we bear the fruit of
God's love. Let us share the joy of our fortune by ex-
changing signs of Christ's peace with one another.

Introduction to the Word (Acts 8:31 NRSV)
When asked by Philip if he really understood the scriptures he was reading, the man replied: "How can I,
unless someone guides me?" As we prepare to read today's scriptures, ask the Holy Spirit to be your guide.
Then, with the Spirit's help, listen for the word of God.

Response to the Word (1 John 4:16b)
 Since God has loved us so completely,
  we also ought to love one another.
 Rejoice in the good news:
  "God is love, and those who remain in love
  remain in God and God remains in them."
 This is good news indeed.

Thanksgiving and Communion

Offering Prayer (Ps 22)
 Bountiful God, you fill the poor with good things
  and cause the hungry to be satisfied.
 May these gifts be instruments of your grace
  and may our very lives be the means
   of spreading your blessings.
 Make these gifts be for the world
  a sign of your boundless love
   and your overflowing abundance. Amen.

Invitation to Communion (1 John 4, John 15)
 Come to the table of grace,
 for Christ is the vine,
 and we are the branches.
  Come, Holy Spirit, come.
 Come to the table of love,
 for whoever does not love,
 does not know God.
  Come, Holy Spirit, come.
 Come to the table of blessing,
 for Christ is here to abide in us,
 as we abide in him.
  Come, Holy Spirit, come.

Sending Forth

Benediction (1 John 4, John 15)
> Beloved, let us love one another,
> for love is from God.
> > **We will be born of love each day of our lives.**
> Beloved, let us abide in Christ's love,
> for he is the vine and we are the branches.
> > **We will grow as Christ's disciples**
> > **and bear fruit for a world in need.**
> Beloved, let us care for one another,
> for the Spirit helps us abide in God's peace.
> > **We will glorify God in the lives we lead.**

May 9, 2021

Sixth Sunday of Easter/Festival of the Christian Home/Mother's Day

Mary Scifres

Copyright © Mary Scifres

Color

White

Scripture Readings

Acts 10:44-48; Psalm 98; 1 John 5:1-6; John 15:9-17

Theme Ideas

When Peter recognized that the Spirit was blessing not just the Jewish followers of Jesus, but Gentiles as well, he proclaimed it loud and clear. There is no confusion for those first followers in the book of Acts: all are invited to God's community. This sounds like a new song for both Judaism and early Christianity, but reach back and remember that the first creation was for all of the earth and all of its peoples. Throughout the ancient psalms, "all the earth" is invited to sing praise to God—all peoples, all creatures, and even the earth itself. This interconnected understanding of creation and humanity expands love beyond the walls of our homes and our churches to invite any and all to the waters of baptism, to the blessings of the Spirit, to the love of God, to the family of love, and to grateful praise for God who creates and blesses us all.

Invitation and Gathering

Centering Words (Ps 98)
Sing praise with all of creation. Sing praise with all of humanity. Sing praise together, for all of our songs come from one God, creator of all.

Call to Worship (Acts 10, Ps 98, 1 John 5, John 15)
Sing a new song,
   a song of love for all.
Sing of the Spirit of love,
   the Spirit who loves us all.
Sing of God's abiding love,
   that we might love one another
   and all of the world.
Sing a new song,
   a song of love for all.

Opening Prayer (Acts 10, Ps 98, 1 John 5, John 15)
Spirit of love, abide in us and in our worship.
Whisper your song of love in our hearts,
   that love may flow through every word we hear,
      every thought we think,
         every word we speak
            and every song we sing.
Spirit of power and grace, abide in us,
   that we may abide in your love
      and proclaim your song of love for all. Amen.

Proclamation and Response

Prayer of Confession (1 John 5, John 15)

Spirit of love, we come in search of love
    and in the hope of learning how to love
        as you love us.
Help us to see others with your eyes of love.
Help us to forgive and accept forgiveness
    as fully and confidently as you forgive.
Love us, dear God, with the mercy and grace we need
    to abide in your love each and every day.
In your love and grace, we pray. Amen.

Words of Assurance (Ps 98, John 15)

God's steadfast love is ours.
God's faithfulness is sure.

–Or–

Words of Assurance (Ps 98, John 15)

God's Spirit is with us,
    embracing us with forgiveness and grace,
    abiding in us with the power of love for all.

Passing the Peace of Christ (1 John 5, John 15)

Loving one another as we have been loved by God, let
us share signs of our love as we pass the peace of Christ
together.

Response to the Word or Opening Prayer (1 John 5, John 15)

Abide in us, Holy Spirit.
Abide in us with your love.
Abide in us with your power.

Abide in us,
    that we might love one another as you love us.
Abide through us,
    that we might love your world,
        as you love the world.
In your love and grace, we pray. Amen.

Thanksgiving and Communion

Offering Prayer (Acts 10, John 15)
Pour out your Holy Spirit on these gifts
    and on all of us gathered here,
        that we may abide in your love
            and that your love may abide in these gifts.
In your loving name, we pray. Amen.

Sending Forth

Benediction (Ps 98, 1 John 5, John 15)
Created by God, we go to love all of creation.
Blessed with love, we are bound by love.
Chosen for love, we go now to love.

May 13, 2021

Ascension Day
Susan Blain

Color

White

Scripture Readings

Acts 1:1-11; Psalm 47; Ephesians 1:15-23; Luke 24:44-53

Theme Ideas

Ascension Day begins a period of waiting for the followers of Jesus. The risen Christ, who has been wonderfully and unexpectedly present with them since Easter—comforting, teaching, challenging—leaves them to
return to the One who sent him into their midst in the
first place. Christ leaves those early followers with many
unanswered questions, but also with the promise that
the Spirit will come to empower them for a future that
they can hardly imagine. The time between Ascension
Day and Pentecost is what we might call a "retreat"—
the time where the disciples gather together to wait and
ponder all that has happened to them, and to prepare for
this new moment in the mission they will share. "Why
are you looking up to heaven?" is the challenge posed to

the disciples by the two strangers in dazzling robes. The prayer, the work, the mission, the very Spirit of Christ is discovered here on earth, in new and surprising ways.

Invitation and Gathering

Centering Words (Acts 1, Luke 24)
Look to the skies. Search for God. Know that God is nearer to us than our very breath.
(B. J. Beu)

Call to Worship (Eph 1)
Mystery of God, draw us near.
Fill our minds with awe!
Wisdom of God, surprise us.
Encourage us with hope!
Glory of God, shine through our lives.
Reveal your power and your glory!
In the mystery, the wisdom, the glory of God,
Let us worship!

Opening Prayer (Acts 1)
Unknowable God, on this most unsettling day,
    you drew Jesus to your side—
        promising his companions Spirit, power,
            mission, and purpose;
        calling his disciples to trust a future
            that they could not yet see.
As we look to Jesus this day,
    give us the same hope of Spirit, power,
        mission and purpose,
            and call to trust a future
                that we too are yet unable to see.

Guide us into your depths,
    that we may glimpse the Spirit
        already at work in our lives—
           revealing your truth
               and empowering us to bear witness
               to the risen Christ.
We pray this in the name of Jesus,
    your Mystery, your Wisdom, your Glory.

Proclamation and Response

Prayer of Confession (Acts 1, Luke 24)

The story of Ascension Day challenges us to seek the presence of the risen Christ in the here and now—in our lives, our community, and our world. Let us pray.

When we "look up to heaven" for our answers,
and so fail to seek the Spirit at work in our midst—
    Lord, have mercy.
When we forget to repent of our wrongdoing;
when we fail to forgive others for mistakes of their own,
and so fail to give witness to the risen Christ—
    Christ, have mercy.
When we doubt the power of your Spirit,
which is at work changing hearts and opening minds,
and so fail to embrace relationships
of righteousness and peace—
    Lord have mercy.

Words of Assurance

Friends, the love of God revealed in Jesus
    Forgives us, heals us, and sets us free
    to witness to his love in the world.

Passing the Peace of Christ (Eph 1)

In the spirit of Paul, who gave thanks for the community's faith in the risen Christ and for their love for one another, let us pass the peace of Christ.

Scripture Ritual

The Christ Candle, symbol of the risen Christ, is traditionally processed out of the sanctuary following the reading of the Ascension Day Gospel. This startling and unsettling ritual makes the point that Jesus must now be present to us in a new way. Have a worship leader bring the Paschal Candle into the center of the Congregation as the Gospel is read, then continue its journey out of the sanctuary after the reading.

Introduction to the Word (Ps 47, The Inclusive Bible)

(As the Christ Candle is taken into the congregation)
God ascended the throne with a shout,
with trumpet blasts!
    Sing praises to God, sing praises.
    Sing praises to our ruler, sing praises!

Response to the Word (Acts 1:11 NRSV)

(After the Christ Candle has been taken out)
As Jesus was going, the disciples gazed toward heaven,
when suddenly two strangers in white robes
stood by them, saying:
    "Why do you stand looking up toward heaven?"

Thanksgiving and Communion

Invitation to the Offering (Luke 24)

Christ calls us to participate in a mission of reconciliation throughout the world—inviting us to participate in the building up of the body of Christ, where justice and peace prevail. Let us give generously of our time, talents, and treasure to foster this mission.

Offering Prayer

O God, we bring to you this offering,
and ask you to bless it and use it
to make your reign known in our world.
In Jesus's name, we pray. Amen

Sending Forth

Benediction (Acts 1, Luke 24)

The disciples looked up to heaven,
and then looked around at each other.
Slowly, understanding dawned upon them
as they began to recognize the presence
of their beloved Jesus in their midst.
With their minds enlightened, and their hearts set free,
they went forth rejoicing, singing and praying,
and waiting for the Spirit's coming.
Let us, too, go forth confident in God.
Let us rejoice in one another,
as we wait in prayer for the surprise of the Spirit.

–Or–

Benediction (Eph 1:17-19, The Inclusive Bible)

"I pray that the God of our Savior Jesus Christ, the God of glory, will give you a spirit of wisdom and revelation, to bring you to a rich knowledge of the Creator.... [May] God...enlighten the eyes of your mind so that you can see the hope this call holds for you—the promised glories that God's Holy Ones will inherit, and the infinitely great power that is exercised for us who believe."

May 16, 2021

Seventh Sunday of Easter/Ascension Sunday
Mary Scifres
Copyright © Mary Scifres

Color

White

Scripture Readings

Acts 1:15-17, 21-26; Psalm 1; 1 John 5:9-13; John 17:6-19

Alternate Scripture Readings for Ascension Day

Acts 1:1-11; Psalm 47; Ephesians 1:15-23; Luke 24:44-53

Theme Ideas

God sends us to serve, but God does not send us alone. The Spirit is with us in the world, guiding our steps and protecting our paths. Christ yearns for us to be one in ministry and service, and one in community and faith—a unity that we discover through the Spirit's miraculous power in our lives. Sent to serve, we are sent not only with the power of the Spirit, but also with the power of unity with one another. Embracing this unity with both the Holy Spirit and one another opens a path to the "complete joy" that Christ prays we may one day know.

Invitation and Gathering

Centering Words (John 17)
    May we all be one.

Call to Worship (Ps 1, John 17)
    To worship and pray,
       we have come this day.
    To meditate on God's teachings,
       we have come this day.
    Gathered as one family of Christ,
       we come together in love.

Opening Prayer (Ps 1, John 17)
    Holy Spirit, be with us in our worship this day.
    Draw us ever closer to you,
       that we may become one.
    Draw us ever closer to your word,
       that we may be wise.
    Draw us ever closer to your world,
       that we may serve and love
          as you guide us to do.
    In your holy name, we pray. Amen.

Proclamation and Response

Prayer of Confession (Ps 1)
    We delight in your law, O God,
       but we don't always follow the rules.
    Shower us with your mercy,
       that we may know your forgiveness
          and your grace.
    Guide our steps,
       that we may follow you more closely.

Draw us ever closer to you and to one another,
that we might support one another
as we follow where you lead us
in our efforts to create a world of unity
and boundless love.
In your mercy and grace, we pray. Amen.

Words of Assurance (Ps 1, John 17)
God watches over us with mercy and grace.
Christ's forgiveness flows freely,
redeeming us and making us whole.

Passing the Peace of Christ (John 17)
Called to be one in Christ Jesus, we are made to love one another in unity and grace. Let's share signs of unity and grace as we pass the peace of Christ with one another this day.

Introduction to the Word (Ps 1)
Listen with love to God's instruction revealed in the scripture we're about to hear.

Response to the Word (Ps 1)
God's word is a gift to nourish our souls,
that we might be like trees
planted by streams of water,
bearing fruit at just the right time,
and living lives of never-fading faith.

Thanksgiving and Communion

Offering Prayer (Ps 1, John 17)
Bless these gifts to be nourishment for a world
hungry for your grace.

Bless us to be nurturers of love
>> for a world hungry for your compassion.
Bless us to be one in ministry with you
>> and with one another,
>>> through the power of your Holy Spirit. Amen.

Sending Forth

Benediction
>> With the power of God's Holy Spirit,
>>> **we have been made one in unity and love.**
>> Even as we go our separate ways,
>>> **we go in unity and love,**
>> We go to serve and love
>>> **with the power of the Spirit.**
>> We go with the blessing of community
>>> **guiding our steps and protecting our paths.**

May 23, 2021

Pentecost Sunday
Karen Clark Ristine

Color
Red

Scripture Readings
Acts 2:1-21; Psalm 104:24-34, 35b; Romans 8:22-27;
John 15:26-27; 16:4b-15

Theme Ideas
Tongues of Fire, Sighs too Deep for Words, Rush of Wind—
this week's scripture readings contain some of the Bible's
greatest hits about the Holy Spirit. This is a day to celebrate Spirit with abandon, drawing on the rich imagery
of advocacy, power, and presence. *(Throughout scripture
the expressions of Spirit are masculine, feminine, and gender-
neutral. Try not to limit your expressions of Spirit with pro-
nouns.)*

Invitation and Gathering

Centering Words (Acts 2, Rom 8, John 15)
Come, Holy Spirit, come. Come as tongues of fire to
enliven us. Come as sighs too deep for words to comfort us. Come as our Advocate to guide us. Come, Holy
Spirit, come.

Call to Worship (Ps 104, John 15)
> Testify to the goodness of God.
>> **Sing praise to God.**
> Testify to the love of Christ.
>> **Sing praise to Christ.**
> Testify to the presence of the Holy Spirit.
>> **Sing praise to Spirit.**

Opening Prayer (Acts 2, Ps 104, Rom 8, John 15)
> Wind of God, present since before creation,
>> fall on us now.
> Whisper to us.
> Shout to us.
> Comfort and guide us.
> Alight on us anew,
>> and revive our own spirits to love and serve.

Proclamation and Response

Prayer of Confession (Rom 8, John 15)
> Gracious God, we do not often listen
>> for your Holy Spirit.
> We turn from your guidance and your inspiration.
> The whispers and the shouts
>> do not penetrate the noise of our daily lives.
> We silence the wisdom available to us
>> through your Spirit of Truth.
> Open our lives to your holy whispers and shouts,
>> that our very lives may testify to unseen hope.
> Amen.

Words of Assurance (John 15)
> In the name of Jesus Christ,
> > who sent us the Spirit of Truth, you are forgiven.
> > **In the name of Jesus Christ, you are forgiven.**

Prayer of Preparation (Acts 2, Ps 104, Rom 8, John 15)
> Come, Holy Spirit, come.
> Open our hearts and minds and lives to your call
> > through this holy word. Amen.

Response to the Word (Acts 2, Ps 104, John 15)
> We hear your call, O God.
> And we will testify.
> We see your presence in all creation.
> We feel the fire of your holy touch.
> We are alive in your Spirit.

Thanksgiving and Communion

Offering Prayer (Rom 8)
> When we do not know how to pray,
> > your Holy Spirit prays for us
> > > in sighs too deep for words.
> Hear our prayers for goodness in the world.
> Receive these gifts,
> > that they may help answer the Holy Spirit's hope
> > > for all creation. Amen.

Invitation to Communion
Come to this table of grace,
where we call on the Holy Spirit
to pour forth on all of us gathered here.
Come and feast and drink deeply
from the cup the Spirit has blessed.

Sending Forth

Benediction (Ps 104)
May the Spirit of God, sent forth to create,
stir in your hearts and minds and souls
a vision of new creation.
Go, Spirit-filled people. Go.

May 30, 2021

First Sunday after Pentecost/Trinity Sunday
Joanne Reynolds

Color

White

Scripture Readings

Isaiah 6:1-8; Psalm 29; Romans 8:12-17; John 3:1-17

Theme Ideas

The themes that link this combination of scripture and the observance of Trinity Sunday together challenge us to renew our understanding of the ways in which we journey with the three persons of the Trinity. This understanding needs to be both solid—the foundation of our faith lives—and fluid because of the sometimes-surprising work of these three aspects of the living God. In so doing, we gain a new perspective of the God of the psalmist and Isaiah as the almighty creator and the authority over all creation. The two other members of the Trinity can likewise provide a fresh way of looking at God's work in the world and our response to it. There's the path to salvation through Jesus that Paul shows us in Romans. Finally, we have Jesus's description of the purpose and work of the Holy Spirit in the Gospel of John.

Invitation and Gathering

Centering Words (John 3:16 NRSV)
"For God so loved the world that he gave his only Son, so that everyone who believes in him may not perish but have everlasting life."

Call to Worship (Ps 29, Isa 6)
Give the Lord glory and power.
Adore the Lord, resplendent and holy.
Holy, holy, holy is the Lord of hosts.
The whole earth is full of God's glory.
Heed the voice of the Lord, full of power.
Regard the voice of the Lord, full of splendor.
Holy, holy, holy is the Lord of hosts.
The whole earth is full of God's glory.
The God of glory thunders.
The Lord's voice flashes flames of fire.
Holy, holy, holy is the Lord of hosts.
The whole earth is full of God's glory.
In God's temple, the people cry, "Glory!"
For the Lord will give strength to the people.
The Lord will bless the people with peace.

–Or–

Call to Worship (John 3, Rom 8)
To see God's kingdom
you must be born from above.
We seek your kingdom, Lord.
To enter God's kingdom
you must be born of water and the Spirit.
We seek your kingdom, Lord.
God sends the Spirit to show us what love is.
We seek your kingdom, Lord.

God sends Jesus to bring us eternal life.
**May we be led by his Spirit, Lord,
and being led, become your children.**

Opening Prayer (Ps 29, John 3, Rom 8)
Creating, all powerful, and triune God,
    we acknowledge your authority as our maker
        to command our obedience.
Loving Jesus, one with humanity,
    and Holy Spirit, living presence of God,
        we thank you for the countless blessings
            you pour into our lives.
Our hearts rejoice, holy one:
    for your infinite love,
        which echoes through creation;
    for Christ's love,
        which came to us in human form;
    for the Spirit's love,
        which calls our hearts
            into fellowship with you.
We bow before you, the Three-in-One,
    and ask that you continue to bless us,
        that we may draw ever closer to you,
            as your children and your heirs. Amen.

Proclamation and Response

Prayer of Confession (Isa 6, John 3, Rom 8)
Almighty God, in our pride,
    we have forgotten your holiness
        and your due as creator of all that is;
    we have failed to care for your creation.
By your grace and mercy, heavenly Father,
    forgive us when we act as if we were your equals.

By your love and compassion, holy Mother,
    correct us when we squander opportunities
        to care for your creation.
Christ, our Savior, through indifference and hatred,
    we have failed to live out your gospel of love
        for all of our sisters and brothers.
By your grace and mercy, beloved Jesus,
    forgive us when we create divisions,
        rather than live in unity and love
           as God's children.
Holy Spirit, in our addiction to busy-ness,
    we have failed to listen for your guidance,
        and have not heeded your call
           to serve God's kingdom.
By your grace and mercy, living Spirit,
    forgive us when we turn a deaf ear to your call
        and when we act as disobedient children. Amen.

Words of Assurance (Rom 8:16-17 NRSV)

God forgives us through an unchanging, enduring love.
Be assured that having received the Spirit,
    we can state with confidence:
    "We are children of God, and if children, then heirs,
    heirs of God and joint heirs with Christ."

Response to the Word (Isa 6)

We give thanks, O Lord,
    that you are one, yet three, in an eternal dance.
We offer you praise, O God,
    that you constantly invite us to dance along,
    even when we feel unworthy.
We hear your call in many ways,
    and through many means,
        as we open our hearts to you.

May we worship you with the seraphs,
and proclaim you as the three that are the Holy One.

Thanksgiving and Communion

Invitation to the Offering (Isa 6:8 NRSV)
Then I heard the voice of the Lord saying, "Whom shall I send, and who will go for us?" And I said, "Here am I; send me!" In light of Isaiah's offering of himself to the Lord, now is the time for us to offer our gifts to God.

Offering Prayer (John 3)
O Lord God, these offerings we make here are tokens;
they represent our love for you.
We thank you for your Spirit's gifts to us,
so mysterious, bountiful, and astounding.
They are blessings upon blessings.
These blessings reveal your presence among us
as the merciful, holy, and loving one. Amen.

Sending Forth

Benediction (Isa 6, Ps 29, Rom 8)
Now go forth with the song of the seraphs in your hearts.
We will praise God's glory and strength.
Depart to rejoin the wayward world we live in.
We will be led by the voice of the Lord.
Go in peace as children of the Almighty Creator,
Thanks be to the Father, Son, and Holy Spirit.

June 6, 2021

Second Sunday after Pentecost, Proper 5
Karin Ellis

Color

Green

Scripture Readings

1 Samuel 8:4-11, (12-15), 16-20; Psalm 138;
2 Corinthians 4:13–5:1; Mark 3:20-35

Theme Ideas

Today's scriptures remind us who is in charge: God.
In the reading from 1 Samuel, we hear how the people wanted a king, someone to rule over them and lead
them into battle. They had forgotten that God rules over
their lives. The psalmist reminds us that God's love is
steadfast, God is always faithful, and God will guide
our lives. Paul tells the Corinthians that the important
things in life—faith, love, the presence of Christ—are
eternal. And Jesus himself reminds us that those who
follow him, who make him the Lord of their lives, are
included in his family. The question to ask this Sunday
is, "Who do we follow as our guide and our savior?"

Invitation and Gathering

Centering Words (Ps 138, 2 Cor 4)

As you enter this sacred space, may you be renewed by the steadfast love of God. May your spirit be filled with the Spirit of Christ, and may you sing praises and give glory to God.

Call to Worship (Ps 138)

People of God, enter this place
with thanksgiving and praise,
    for the Lord is good.
Come and rejoice, sing glory to God,
    for the Lord is good.
Remember, the steadfast love of God endures forever,
    for the Lord is good.

Opening Prayer (2 Cor 4, Mark 3:35 NRSV)

Loving God, some of us come to this place
    full of anticipation and joy,
        others come weary and tired.
And some of us come here today
    wondering why we are even here.
Renew us in your Holy Spirit.
Remind us that your steadfast love
    follows us wherever we go.
Increase our faith,
    that we may not lose heart
        or become burdened by the challenges of life.
Help us hear again the words of Christ:
    "Whoever does the will of God
        is my brother and sister and mother."
We are yours, O God.

Thank you for claiming us as your own.
In the name of Christ, your Son and our savior,
   we pray. Amen.

Proclamation and Response

Prayer of Confession (1 Sam, 2 Cor 4)
Gracious God, we often forget
   that you are the ruler of our lives.
Instead, we turn our attention elsewhere.
We want what others have.
We allow the concerns of the world to weigh us down.
We become distracted by the activities around us.
We forget to keep our focus on you.
Forgive us.
Strengthen our faith,
   that we may see your presence in our lives.
Remind us again that you are the Lord of our lives—
   the one who loves us completely,
   the one who offers us abundant forgiveness,
   the one who never leaves our side.
In your holy name we pray. Amen.

Words of Assurance (Ps 138)
Brothers and sisters, the hand of God
   stretches far and wide to forgive us,
   bringing us newness of life.
In the name of God, whose love endures forever,
   you are forgiven.
Thanks be to God!

Passing the Peace of Christ (Mark 3)
The peace of Christ be with you.
   And also with you.

With an outstretched hand, and an open heart, I invite you to greet one another as brothers and sisters, as mothers and fathers.

Prayer of Preparation (2 Cor 4, Mark 3)
Holy One, open our hearts to your loving Spirit.
Incline our ears to the truth of your scriptures.
Renew our lives in thanksgiving and praise. Amen.

Response to the Word (Ps 138, 2 Cor 4, Mark 3)
People of God, do you feel the movement
of the Holy Spirit?
>   **Our hearts have been broken open
>   to receive the grace of God.**
People of God, what do you hear?
>   **We hear Christ calling us to follow
>   and to be faithful.**
People of God, will you renew your lives
in the word of God?
>   **We will, with thanksgiving and praise;
>   and we will sing the song of God.**
Praise be to God!
>   **Praise be to Christ!**

Thanksgiving and Communion

Invitation to the Offering (1 Sam 8, Ps 138)
We have come to give praise to God and to say thank you for all that God has given us. In thanksgiving and praise, let us bring our gifts before God.

Offering Prayer (Ps 138, 2 Cor 4)
Almighty Creator, you have blessed us
>   with abundant life and steadfast love.

We offer these gifts to you,
    asking that your Holy Spirit will bless them
        and use them to shower grace and love
           upon our brothers and sisters,
              both near and far.
In the name of Christ, we pray. Amen.

Sending Forth

Benediction (2 Cor 4)
    Brothers and sisters, as you go from this place:
        extend grace to all,
        be faithful to Christ,
        and do not lose hope.
    Go in peace. Amen.

June 13, 2021

Third Sunday after Pentecost, Proper 6
B. J. Beu and Mary Scifres
Copyright © B. J. Beu and Mary Scifres

Color

Green

Scripture Readings

1 Samuel 15:34–16:13; Psalm 20; 2 Corinthians 5:6-10, (11-13), 14-17; Mark 4:26-34

Theme Ideas

It is only with the heart that one can see rightly. This truth is witnessed in God's decision to anoint David as the new king of Israel: "the Lord does not see as mortals see; they look on the outward appearance, but the Lord looks on the heart" (1 Sam 16:7b NRSV). This truth is proclaimed by Paul in his insistence: "We walk by faith, not by sight" (2 Cor 5:7 NRSV). And it is expressed by Jesus as he compares the kingdom of God to a tiny mustard seed where birds will one day make their nests. These scriptures teach us to see with the heart, that God may grant us our hearts' true desire.

Invitation and Gathering

Centering Words (2 Cor 5, Eph 1)

See as God sees. Only then can we see rightly. Love as God loves. Only then can we love with the eyes of our heart enlightened.

Call to Worship (Ps 20, 2 Cor 5, Mark 4)

Come, walk in the light of faith.
We will walk humbly with our God.
Come, love in the light of faith.
We will love everything the light touches.
Come, sing in the light of faith.
We will sing praise to our God.
Come, live in the light of faith.
We will live as faithful followers of Christ.

Opening Prayer (1 Sam 15–16, Mark 4)

Help us to walk by faith, O God,
    not by sight.
Be our vision, Holy One,
    for without vision your people perish.
Remind us that you do not see as mortals see,
    for you do not judge by outward appearances,
        but look on the heart.
With our eyes of faith enlightened,
    help us see your kingdom in a tiny mustard seed,
        and marvel at the growth you offer to all
            through the power of your Spirit. Amen.

Proclamation and Response

Prayer of Yearning (1 Sam 16, Mark 4)
When death comes, we yearn for your grace
and the healing you offer
in the midst of our grief.
When tragedy strikes, we long for your mercy
and the blessed assurance you offer
in midst of our suffering.
When trouble threatens, we look for your shelter
and the confidence you offer
in the midst of our confusion and doubt.
Renew our trust in your resurrection,
and revive our hope in new beginnings.
As Samuel before us,
help us focus on life, listen to your voice,
and follow where you lead.
In your holy name, we pray. Amen.

Words of Assurance (Ps 20, 2 Cor 5)
As we allow God to shape the desires of our hearts,
we live and move in concert with God's plans.
Rejoice that in Christ we have become a new creation
and agents to bring forth the reign of God.

Passing the Peace of Christ (2 Cor 5)
When we see with the eyes of God, we perceive that
each person here is a new creation, planted by God and
rooted in Christ. As we share signs of peace and love,
take time to really look at one another and rejoice in the
new life all around us.

Invitation to the Word (1 Sam 15–16, 2 Cor 5)

The one who calls us to walk by faith, not by sight, is here to open our hearts, that we may hear the word of God. The one who judges the heart, not outward appearances, is present to guide our ears, that we may hear what is truly the word of God.

Response to the Word (2 Cor 5)

God shows us the path of faith before our feet.
We travel familiar ground.
With the eyes of our hearts enlightened,
follow the journey of faith with confidence.
We travel the road of the saints.
Walk by faith, not by sight,
for it is only with the heart that one can see rightly.
We travel with Christ, who is our path.

Thanksgiving and Communion

Offering Prayer (Mark 4)

Bountiful God, your kingdom is like seed
that is scattered on the ground.
How it grows, we know not,
but there is abundance in the harvest.
Your kingdom is like a tiny mustard seed
that grows into a shrub,
where the birds of the air
build their nests.
May the gifts we bring before you this day
bear the fruit of your kingdom,
where all may be fed,
and all may be blessed. Amen.

Sending Forth

Benediction (1 Sam 15, 2 Cor 5, Mark 4)
Go forth to proclaim the good news
that we are new creations in Christ Jesus.
As seeds planted by God,
we go to spread God's gifts of love and hope.
Go forth to live the good news
that we live in a time of new beginnings.
As plantings of the Lord,
we go to share God's gifts of mercy and grace.

June 20, 2021

Fourth Sunday after Pentecost, Proper 7/Father's Day

B. J. Beu

Copyright © B. J. Beu

Color

Green

Scripture Readings

1 Samuel 17:(1a, 4-11, 19-23), 32-49; Psalm 9:9-20;
2 Corinthians 6:1-13; Mark 4:35-41

Theme Ideas

Battles, vengeance, adversity, and suffering are plentiful in today's readings. Those seeking an alternative theme might consider this subtheme: the power of the unexpected and the surprising. An elder King Saul takes a chance on a confident, young David, who wisely sheds conventional armor. In Psalm 9, God takes the side of the oppressed, needy, and poor, and is asked to declare nations as "only human." In rebuking a storm, Jesus speaks the word *peace*. In a dispute with the Corinthians, Paul issues an appeal to and from the heart.

141

Invitation and Gathering

Centering Words (2 Cor 6)
> With God, all things are possible. Rejoice, for this is the day of our salvation.

Call to Worship (Ps 9)
> Sing praises to the Lord, sing praises.
> **We will declare God's deeds among the people.**
> Shout for joy, you children of the Most High.
> **God remembers the needy**
> **and gives hope to the poor.**
> Sing praises to the Lord, sing praises.
> **We will declare God's deeds among the people.**

Opening Prayer (1 Sam 17, Ps 9, 2 Cor 6, Mark 4)
> When the storms of life crash around us, O God,
>> be our quiet center.
> When adversaries gather against us, Holy One,
>> be our refuge and our strength.
> Give us the confidence of David,
>> that we might place our trust entirely in you.
> And give us the assurance of the psalmist,
>> that we might know the glory of our salvation.
> With joyful hearts and ready minds,
>> we pray for your grace this day. Amen.

Proclamation and Response

Prayer of Yearning (Mark 4:39a NRSV)
> Merciful God, be with us in our hour of need.
> When lashed by the winds of life,
>> we long to hear you speak words of grace,
>>> "Peace! Be still!"

When frightened by the waves of woe,
    we yearn to have you by our side,
        calming our fear.
Reveal your Presence in the eye of the storm,
    and give us the courage to call out in our need,
        for you are our calm center
           and our hope when all hope seems lost.

Words of Assurance (2 Cor 6)

God listens; God helps. Now is the day of our salvation.
Rejoice and receive the good news.

Passing the Peace of Christ (Mark 4)

With a word, Christ calmed the waters when the disciples were in peril. A word of peace can have awesome power. Let us share signs of this peace with one another.

Invitation to the Word (Mark 4, 2 Cor 6)

Gracious God, great Teacher, bearer of peace,
    we come today seeking your wisdom.
Open our ears to hear your word,
    and open our hearts to perceive possibilities,
    seen and unseen. Amen.

Response to the Word (1 Sam 17, Ps 9, 2 Cor 6, Mark 4)

You're not what we expect, O Lord:
    victory without a sword,
    windstorms calmed with a mere word of peace,
    sleepless nights rewarded.
Help us place our hope and trust firmly in you,
    that our lives may bear the fruit of faithful living
    and hopeful promise. Amen.

Thanksgiving and Communion

Offering Prayer (1 Sam 17)
Merciful God, we thank you for the example
of those who have walked before us in faith.
May the offering of our ministries
nurture the young in our midst,
just as David was nurtured by Saul.
May the offerings of our lives
honor those you seek to help and defend.
Accept our gifts, we pray,
and bless now this morning's offerings,
that we might do your will
wherever we are called to serve. Amen.

Sending Forth

Benediction (2 Cor 6)
Go with the blessings of almighty God:
purity, knowledge, patience, kindness,
holiness of spirit, genuine love, truthful speech,
and the power of our Lord.
Go in peace and be a blessing
for everyone you meet.

June 27, 2021

Fifth Sunday after Pentecost, Proper 8
Kirsten Linford

Color

Green

Scripture Readings

2 Samuel 1:1, 17-27; Psalm 130; 2 Corinthians 8:7-15; Mark 5:21-43

Theme Ideas

In various ways, these lections focus on seeking hope in the midst of loss: the loss of loved ones in the Samuel passage; the movement from grief to hope in the psalm; losses of life for a young girl and health for a bleeding woman in the Gospel, as well as the hope of healing from Jesus; and Paul's reminder that it is often through Christ's losses that we find hope and abundance. Expressions of grief and expressions of hope are both acts of faith, for we would not bother to call out to God if we didn't hope and believe that God would hear and respond.

Invitation and Gathering

Centering Words (Ps 130)

Out of the depths, we cry to God. How do we seek hope in the wake of loss, in the midst of grief? How can our souls wait for the Lord like those who wait for the morning?

Call to Worship (Ps 130)

We wait for the Lord, our souls wait for the Lord,
 and find hope in God's word.
Our souls wait for the Lord
 more than those who watch for the morning.
More than those who watch for the morning.
 Let us seek hope in our God,
whose power is enduring love,
 whose redemption brings healing and grace.
We wait for the Lord,
 and find our hope in God's presence.

Opening Prayer (Ps 130)

Holy One, in peace or in pain,
 we call to you,
  and you answer.
Hear our voices, O God,
 and the cries of our hearts.
Come and bring us your presence.
Come and bring us your peace. Amen.

Proclamation and Response

Prayer of Confession (Mark 5)

God of Grace, we come to you in search of healing.
We come to you in search of peace.

We come, often bearing only a tiny seed of hope within,
    praying that it is enough.
Our cries come in the deepest part of the night,
    and we do not always ask for help.
Our hearts bleed just as surely as our bodies,
    and we do not always recognize
        the hidden pain of others.
Or even our own.
Sometimes we struggle to find our faith at all,
    and forget that doubt, too, is a part of belief.
Give us courage enough
    to reach out for the hem of your cloak.
Give us strength enough
    to speak the truth of our own struggles,
        and to see and hear and know
           the struggles of others.
Forgive us when we think you only want us
    if we're perfect.
Fill us with your endless supply of love,
    so that we might try again. Amen.

Words of Assurance (2 Cor 8, Mark 5)
Christ gave us his weakness,
    that we might become strong.
He gave us the wealth of his wisdom,
    that we might know what is true.
He offered his own vulnerability,
    making himself defenseless,
    that we might actually learn love.
It is the faith Christ has given us
    that has made us well;
the power of God's love
    that heals and redeems.
There is forgiveness in God,
    and a hope that makes us whole.

Passing the Peace of Christ (Mark 5)

Having received Christ's peace, we share signs of it now with one another. For God's healing is meant to move both within us and between us.

Prayer of Preparation (Ps 19)

May the words of my mouth...
> and the meditations of our hearts
> > be acceptable in your sight, O Lord,
> > > our strength and our redeemer. Amen.

Response to the Word (Mark 5)

God of Mercy, you believe in us,
> and offer us love to change our lives.
Help us now believe in you,
> whether fearful and trembling
> > or confidently at peace.
May your word be alive in our souls,
> so that hope may not die,
> > but only sleep for awhile,
> > > waiting to awake.

Thanksgiving and Communion

Offering Prayer (Ps 130, Mark 5)

Gracious One, you have given us a love
> that stretches farther than we can see
> > or even believe.
You have given us a grace and a forgiveness
> that is deeper than our vulnerabilities.
You have given us a healing and a hope
> that makes us whole.
Take now the offerings of our hearts and our lives,
> even as we give away all you have given us. Amen.

Sending Forth

Benediction (Ps 130, Mark 5)
> We have waited for the Lord,
>> and God has not failed us.
> We have reached for Christ,
>> and he has met us where we are.
> Go in peace, to love and to serve,
>> healed and free.

July 4, 2021

Sixth Sunday after Pentecost, Proper 9
Michelle L. Torigian

Color

Green

Scripture Readings

2 Samuel 5:1-5, 9-10; Psalm 48; 2 Corinthians 12:2-10; Mark 6:1-13

Theme Ideas

What is our identity? Whether our identity as individuals, as congregations, as communities, or as other organizations, we are given the opportunity to solidify who we are—especially in our relationship to the divine. For both David and Jesus, it was their sense of call. Second Samuel recalls that David "was thirty years old when he began to reign" (v. 4 NRSV), and the text establishes a sense of authority for David's monarchy. Faced with questions, Jesus establishes his authority in his hometown, looking beyond the boundary of his family structure to his identity in God. In this collection of texts, whether we are in times of victory or vulnerability, God is with us. We find our strength, identity, and sense of call through God, as seen in Jesus the Christ.

Invitation and Gathering

Centering Words (Ps 48, 2 Cor 12, Mark 6)
With each breath we take, our spirits breathe in God's Spirit. Our souls rejoice in the one who fully knows our hearts. God's grace sustains us, even in the midst of our weaknesses. As we exhale, let us reflect upon our relationships with our neighbors. The same Spirit that energizes us nourishes our neighbors. Pondering God's steadfast love, may we see the ways that God is calling us in this space and time.

Call to Worship (Ps 48, 2 Cor 12)
When winds tear into our vessels,
God's grace will be our guide.
When insecurities mount up within our souls,
God's strength will be our guide.
When hardships weaken our resolve,
God's mercy will be our guide.
When insults rip and slander stains,
God's courage will be our guide.
When vulnerability saps our faith,
God's presence will be our guide.

Opening Prayer (2 Cor 12, Ps 48, 2 Sam 5, Mark 6)
Divine Summoner, through your voice,
we understand who you created us to be.
Through your voice,
we understand our calling.
Through your persistent presence,
we find resilience.
May we contently embrace our vulnerabilities.
May we boldly claim our pasts,
and may we find our future
with determination and grace. Amen.

Proclamation and Response

Prayer of Confession (Mark 6)

> Holy Creator, we have refused to give our neighbors
>> the honor they deserve.
> We have rejected others,
>> as Jesus was rejected before us.
> Status drives us.
> Gossip lures us.
> Reputations gain more traction
>> than the entirety of the person in front of us.
> We choose chaos over kindness,
>> and disconnection over spiritual bonds.
> May our hearts repent,
>> returning to your voice.
> May our souls reconnect,
>> returning to our neighbor.
> May our minds renew,
>> returning to the ones you created us to be.
> May your grace abound. Amen.

Words of Assurance (2 Cor 12)

> Shame lives within us no more.
> God's grace is sufficient for all.
> May the power of Christ dwell in our souls,
>> elevate our spirits, and nudge us to grow
>> in our relationships. Amen.

Passing of the Peace of Christ (2 Cor 12)

> Greet one another, and look deeply into the eyes of your
> neighbors. See the glorious vulnerability of our siblings
> around us. Know in your bones that we are all contrib-
> uting our best to this life, and we are all rejoicing in the
> grace of God when we fall short.

Response to the Word (2 Sam 5, Ps 48, 2 Cor 12, Mark 6)

Take a moment to find the Divine's image within you.

For some of us, the image may seem unfamiliar.

Take a moment to silently name your insecurities.

For some of us, these weaknesses seem intense.

Take a moment to prayerfully claim your identity
in God.

For some of us, assertions of authenticity are new.

Whether we feel vulnerable or victorious,

God walks alongside of us.

Whether we are fragile or robust,

**God's steadfast love shines brightly
in our hearts.**

Thanksgiving and Communion

Invitation to Offering (2 Sam 5, Ps 48, Mark 6)

God calls us to serve and invites us to give. Knowing
that God will be guiding us, and that God will be leading us, let us claim the generosity of God. In our celebration of this bounty, we share our treasures, talents, and
time with the church and community.

Offering Prayer (Ps 48, 2 Cor 12, Mark 6)

Despite the sufferings and challenges on our journeys,
your power transcends human weakness.

We celebrate your generosity by sharing treasures,
talents, and time along our way.

No matter where we travel or which hardships we face,
we sing your name in every corner of the earth.

With our songs of praise,
we share our gifts with your creation. Amen.

Communion Prayer (Ps 48, 2 Cor 12, Mark 6)
Great is God's name.
And great is the table of Christ.
As we approach this meal,
we ponder the steadfast love of God.
We praise God's name
in each corner of the earth.

Great Thanksgiving
In our times of victory or vulnerability,
there are seats for us all.
Regardless of our painful pasts,
the thorns in our bodies,
or the insults plunged into our souls,
there are places for each of us at this meal.
No matter which neighbor or kin
have turned their backs on us,
no matter how many tears have fallen from our eyes,
we each are welcome here.
At this meal, we once again find our strength.
At the table of Christ, we renew our energy.

The night before Jesus faced rejection and desertion,
persecution and insults, he joined with friends
to share a meal.
This meal fed Jesus, not only in body,
but also in mind and soul.
"Remember me," he instructed his companions.
"Remember me," he spoke,
as he shared the bread and cup.

In this time and space, as God's Spirit encircles us,
Christ continues to abide with us.

Christ stirs us to widen the table,
    nudging us to add a chair,
    or to take this feast to someone missing today.
And as we expand the sacred meal of Christ,
    we remember him.
We remember the night he celebrated with friends.
We remember the day he was rejected and deserted.
We remember the morning he emerged from the tomb.
And we find our strength in his resurrection. Amen.

Sending Forth

Benediction (2 Sam 5, Ps 48, 2 Cor 12, Mark 6)
Let us delight in the steadfast love of God,
    as we share our weaknesses
    or celebrate our strengths.
Let us rejoice in God's glory,
    as we rejoice in our individual
    and our communal callings.
Let us sing of God's name,
    as we journey throughout God's great earth.
Let us remember God, who guides our path,
    the Christ who strengthens us,
    and the Spirit who nurtures us.
May the divine image dance within us forevermore.
Amen.

July 11, 2021

Seventh Sunday after Pentecost, Proper 10
Mary Scifres
Copyright © Mary Scifres

Color

Green

Scripture Readings

2 Samuel 6:1-5, 12b-19; Psalm 24; Ephesians 1:3-14; Mark 6:14-29

Theme Ideas

What if every follower of God understood the opportunity we are given to be an honor to God's glory? What if each of our words praised God's glory? Ephesians 1:12 invites us to see ourselves this way, and the psalmist invites us to recognize that we belong to God alongside all of God's creation. David sings and dances praise to God, but Michal resents him for doing so. Herod respects John the Baptist, but allows his daughter to turn her lovely dance into a demand for John's death. Honoring God's glory in our very being and praising God's glory with our every word and action prevents such misuse of our lives, even as it opens the door for praise, gratitude, and discipleship—qualities we hope to guide our steps and to define our lives.

Invitation and Gathering

Centering Words (Eph 1)
May our lives be an honor and glory to God, who is our
hope and our salvation.

Call to Worship (2 Sam 6, Ps 24, Eph 1)
The earth is God's and everything in it.
We belong to our God.
Lift up your voices in praise and thanksgiving.
We lift our voices in glory and honor to God.

Opening Prayer (2 Sam 6, Eph 1)
God of grace and glory,
renew us with your presence this day.
As we gather to bless your name and sing your praise,
bless us with your glorious love
and your guiding light.
Strengthen us each and every hour,
through the power of your Holy Spirit
and the wisdom of your holy word.
In hope and joy, we pray. Amen.

Proclamation and Response

Prayer of Confession (2 Sam 6, Eph 1, Mark 6)
Gracious God, pour out your mercy on us.
Where there is despair,
fill us with hope.
Where there is sorrow,
fill us with comfort.
Where there is sin,
fill us with forgiveness.

Where there is hatred,
    fill us with love.
Where there is worry,
    fill us with assurance.
Gather us in the arms of your grace and glory,
    that we may reflect your glory
        with honor and praise
            all the days of our lives.
In your holy name, we pray. Amen.

Words of Assurance (Ps 24, Eph 1)

God, who saves, is amongst us now:
    filling our lives with grace,
    forgiving us and making us one,
    perfecting all of creation,
        through the mercy of God's steadfast love.

Passing the Peace of Christ (Eph 1)

Called to be an honor to God's glory, let's honor one another with signs of peace and with words of love.

Introduction to the Word (Eph 1)

Listen for the word of truth
    in the scripture offered this day.

Response to the Word (Eph 1)

Invited to be an honor to God's glory,
    **we can become reflections of God's glorious love
    and grace.**
Invited to sing praise to God's glory,
    **we can become voices of God's hope
    for all the world.**

Thanksgiving and Communion

Invitation to the Offering (2 Sam 6, Eph 1)
With what shall we bring our praise and honor to God?
As we bring offerings and gifts this day, we are invited
to reflect on the myriad ways we might offer our words,
our actions, our lives, and our very being in praise and
honor to God.

Offering Prayer (2 Sam 6, Ps 24, Eph 1)
Glorious God, we thank you for trusting us
    to reflect your glory.
For claiming us as your own with all of creation,
    we give you thanks and praise.
As you receive these gifts and offerings,
    receive us also.
Blessing all together,
    that our gifts and our lives might be a blessing
        that honors and glorifies you.

Sending Forth

Benediction (Eph 1, Eph 5)
Brilliant children of light,
go now to shine with God's glory and love.
We will shine brightly and love freely.
Honor God with all that you say and do.
**We will make the world a better
and a brighter place for all to live.**

July 18, 2021

Eighth Sunday after Pentecost, Proper 11

Mary Scifres
Copyright © Mary Scifres

Color

Green

Scripture Readings

2 Samuel 7:1-14a; Psalm 89:20-37; Ephesians 2:11-22;
Mark 6:30-34, 53-56

Theme Ideas

God dwells in the people of God's creation, not in buildings or houses. The way we live reveals the Spirit's presence in our world. The way we lead reveals God's guidance in our lives. The dynasties we build are valuable
only in as much as they build God's realm on this earth.
Each of today's scriptures points to the power of God's
indwelling in the lives of people. Whether we are leading
a nation, building a community, creating reconciliation
between different factions, healing people in need, teaching God's love, or inviting people to rest in that love, we
are revealing God's presence with our very lives. Building lives on Christ our cornerstone, we are building a dy-
nasty of God's steadfast love and faithfulness.

Invitation and Gathering

Centering Words (Eph 2)

From far and near, we gather to be close to God. But always, God dwells in and with us. No matter how far we wander, God's Spirit is as near to us as our very breath.

Call to Worship (Ps 89, Eph 2)

From far and near, we gather together,
called to unity in Christ.
Built into one body,
we are the dwelling place of God.
May God guide our steps and direct our ways,
that we may reveal God's love in word and deed.

Opening Prayer (Ps 89, Eph 2)

Holy Spirit, flow through our worship.
Dwell in us this day and all days.
Speak through our words,
    breathe into our thoughts,
        and gather us together
            as one community of faith.
Build us together
    on the foundation that is ours in Christ Jesus
        our cornerstone.
Flow through our days,
    that we may be reflections of your presence.
In your holy name, we pray. Amen.

Proclamation and Response

Prayer of Confession (2 Sam 7, Eph 2, Mark 6)
> Guiding, guardian God,
>> we do not want to be like sheep without a shepherd,
>>> or strangers wandering alone in the world.
>
> We want to know your presence,
>> and trust that you dwell within us.
>
> We yearn for conviction that your Spirit
>> flows in and through us.
>
> Fill us when we are empty.
>
> Forgive us when we are wrong.
>
> Guide us when we are lost.
>
> Comfort us when we are tired.
>
> Reconcile us when we are disconnected,
>> and guard our lives with your indwelling Spirit.
>
> In your loving name, we pray. Amen.

Words of Assurance (Eph 2)
> Christ is our peace, reconciling us with God
>> and with one another.
>
> In our very lives, Christ dwells, full of mercy and grace
>> to draw us to the heart of God.

Passing the Peace of Christ (Eph 2)
> In Christ, who is our peace, we live and love. As Christ's
> sisters and brothers, let us be at peace with one another.
> Turn to a sister or brother and share the peace of Christ
> that dwells within.

Response to the Word (2 Sam 7, Ps 89, Eph 2, Mark 6)
> Father God, Mother Spirit, Rock of our salvation,
>> hear our prayer.

Guard us when we are in danger.
Guide us when we wander.
Dwell in us so fully
that we may remember who we are
and whose we are.
In your mercy and grace, we pray. Amen.

Thanksgiving and Communion

Offering Prayer (Eph 2, Mark 6)
Holy Spirit, flow through these gifts
we return to you now.
Dwell in them, as you dwell in us,
that others may know your abiding presence
and your steadfast love.
In your holy presence, we pray. Amen.

Sending Forth

Benediction (Eph 2)
From far and near, we have been brought close
to one another in the heart of God.
As we wander forth in the world,
may we remember that God dwells in us,
and that God's Spirit is as near to us
as our very breath.

July 25, 2021

Ninth Sunday after Pentecost, Proper 12
B. J. Beu
Copyright © B. J. Beu

Color

Green

Scripture Readings

2 Samuel 11:1-15; Psalm 14; Ephesians 3:14-21;
John 6:1-21

Theme Ideas

We can be as thick as bricks sometimes. Fools say in their hearts, "There is no God." And even King David succumbs to the worst version of himself as he commits adultery with Bathsheba and has her husband killed in battle. We are called to celebrate with Paul that all the families of the earth take their name in God, and that we discover God's love in Christ. Finally, we are called to have an encounter with the one who feeds us and gathers up the fragments of our lives, that nothing may be lost.

Invitation and Gathering

Centering Words (Ps 14:1a)

Fools say in their hearts: "There is no God." The faithful prove the foolishness of these words, not with their words, but with their actions.

Call to Worship (John 6)

Why have you come to this place?

We are tired in body and spirit.

Why have you come today?

We have come to follow Jesus.

Come and eat your fill.

But there are only five barley loaves and two fish.

There is plenty for all.

Jesus gathers the fragments of our lives,
that nothing may be lost.

Come! Let us worship.

Opening Prayer (Ps 14)

God of steadfast love, fools say in their hearts:
"There is no God."
May our words and our very lives
prove that we are not foolish.
May our faith be as constant as the North Star,
and may others know that we are Christians
by our love. Amen.

Proclamation and Response

Prayer of Yearning (John 6)
God of our hopes and dreams,
>   we are empty, and long to be filled;
>   we are hungry, and long to be fed;
>   we are lost, and long to be found.
Invite us once more to eat our fill
>   and find our true nourishment in Jesus,
>   the bread of heaven.
Just as Jesus gathered up the fragments
>   of the five loaves and two fish
>   after feeding the five thousand,
>   gather up the pieces of our lives
>   and shelter us in your love. Amen.

Words of Assurance (Ps 14)
As God restored the fortunes of Zion,
>   exiles were like people who dream—
>   people filled with rejoicing and gladness.
As God restores our fortunes,
>   let us join their glad song and their rejoicing.

Passing the Peace of Christ (Eph 3)
In response to the love we have found in Christ—a love
that passes all understanding—let us share signs of
Christ's peace.

Introduction to the Word (Eph 3:18-19 NRSV)
Hear anew the words of Paul: "I pray that you may have
the power to comprehend, with all the saints, what is the
breadth and length and height and depth, and to know
the love of Christ that surpasses knowledge, so that you
may be filled with all the fullness of God."

Response to the Word (Eph 3)

As God strengthens us in our inner being,
may we know the glory of God's Spirit.
As God stirs within us this day,
may we be filled with the knowledge of God.

–Or–

Response to the Word (Eph 3, John 6)

Jesus feeds us in our need.
We are sustained by God's loving Spirit.
Jesus brings us hope.
We are strengthened by God's mercy and grace.
Jesus gathers the lost and the scattered.
We are reclaimed by God's saving love.
In Jesus, we are made whole.

Thanksgiving and Communion

Offering Prayer (John 6)

Caretaker of our souls,
in your love, nothing is lost.
As Jesus gathered the leftover food
after feeding the five thousand,
gather our offerings into your service.
As Jesus gathered the longing of those
who looked to him to be their king,
gather our longing to do your will.
As Jesus gathered the outcasts
to your heavenly banquet,
gather our fellowship into your host of saints.
Bless the gifts we have gathered in your name,
that nothing may be lost,
and that everything may be gained. Amen.

Sending Forth

Benediction (John 6)

> Go to follow Jesus,
>> who gives us the bread of life.
>
> Go to walk in the ways of Christ,
>> who strengthens us in our inner being
>> through the power of the Holy Spirit.
>
> Go to serve our living Lord,
>> who gathers the fragments of our lives,
>> that nothing may be lost.

August 1, 2021

Tenth Sunday after Pentecost, Proper 13
Mary Scifres
Copyright © Mary Scifres

Color

Green

Scripture Readings

2 Samuel 11:26–12:13a; Psalm 51:1-12; Ephesians 4:1-16;
John 6:24-35

Theme Ideas

How might we live as people worthy of God's call in our
lives? David faced a cruel reality when Nathan brought
to light the error of his ways with Uriah and Bathsheba:
Even the greatest of God's followers can fall from grace if
they lose sight of God's call in their lives; even the wisest
can stumble when they shirk the responsibility to live as
people worthy of that call. Speaking the truth in love, Nathan brings this reality to David's attention and calls him
back to living in a worthy manner. The letter to the Ephesians, particularly these last three chapters, has much to
teach us about how we can live in this worthy manner. Jesus reminds us throughout the sixth chapter of John that

God offers us the spiritual nourishment we need in order to live this way. The nourishment and gifts we receive from God are blessings, as they were for David. But these are blessings meant to strengthen us as disciples, that we might bless and strengthen others. In this way, we can indeed live as people worthy of the call we have received.

Invitation and Gathering

Centering Words (Eph 4)

Encourage one another to live as people worthy of God's calling.

Call to Worship (Eph 4)

As one body of Christ,
we gather together this day.
Blessed by one Spirit,
we gather in unity and love.

Opening Prayer (2 Sam 11–12, Ps 51, Eph 4)

Speak truth to us this day, O God.
Speak truth to the most inward parts
of our hearts and minds,
that we might speak your truth in love
and that you might speak your truth through us
each and every day.
In your holy name, we pray. Amen.

Proclamation and Response

Prayer of Confession (2 Sam 11–12, Ps 51, Eph 4)
    Gracious God, we want to live as people
        worthy of your calling.
    Help us recognize your gifts and blessings,
        that we may live up to our calling
            and bless others with our words and our lives.
    When we fall short,
        have mercy on us.
    When we don't know our mistakes,
        speak truth to us with your loving guidance.
    Create a new heart within us,
        a heart full of love and gratitude.
    Nourish us with the grace of your presence,
        that we may indeed live as people
            worthy of your calling. Amen.

Words of Assurance (Ps 51, John 6)
    In Christ's grace, our hearts are cleansed
        and our lives are made whole.
    In Christ's grace, we are forgiven and loved for life.

Passing the Peace of Christ (Eph 4)
    Accept one another with love, as we have been accepted
    with love. In the unity of God's Spirit, let us exchange
    signs of Christ's peace.

Introduction to the Word (Eph 4, John 6)
    God seeks to guide us into mature adulthood.
    Listen for God's nourishing word,
        that we may grow in the knowledge
        and the love of Christ.

Response to the Word: An Affirmation of Faith (Eph 4)
(You may read this in unison or responsively.)
As people worthy of God's calling
we recommit to living this call:
by conducting ourselves with humility,
gentleness, and patience;
by making every effort to preserve our unity,
and accepting one another with love,
and by celebrating our various gifts,
that we may grow in every way into Christ.

Thanksgiving and Communion

Invitation to the Offering (Eph 4)
Whatever measure of grace and giftedness you have
been given, it is enough. From this measure, you are
invited to share yourselves with God and with God's
world.

Offering Prayer (Eph 4, John 6)
For calling us into ministry with you,
we give you thanks and praise, O God.
For gracing us with gifts and abundance,
we are ever grateful.
Bless these gifts we now dedicate to you,
that they may nourish others
with the grace of your presence.
In gratitude, we pray. Amen.

Great Thanksgiving
The bread of life be with you.
And also with you.
Lift up your hearts.
We lift them up to God.

Let us give thanks to the God of love and grace.
It is right to give God our thanks and praise.

It is right, and a good and joyful thing,
    to bring our thanks and gratitude to you,
    God of love and grace.
Since the beginning of time,
    you have created us in your image,
    nourished us with your wisdom and grace,
    called us into relationship with you,
    and invited us to live lives worthy
    of your calling.
When we failed to live in a manner
    worthy of this calling,
    and when we wandered lost on the paths
    of death and destruction,
    you continued to walk with us,
    nourishing us with your wisdom and grace.
In the words of prophets and poets,
    you have spoken your truth in love,
    reminding us of your call,
    and showing us the way to answer it.
In the fullness of time,
    you came to us as the bread of life,
    as Jesus the Christ,
    speaking truth in new and renewing ways,
    calling us to unity and peace,
    showering us with mercy and grace,
    and inviting us to live as your people on earth.
And so, with your people on earth,
    and all the company of heaven,
    we praise your name
    and join their unending hymn, saying:

**Holy, holy, holy Lord, God of power and might,
heaven and earth are full of your glory.
Hosanna in the highest. Blessed is the one
who comes in the name of the Lord.
Hosanna in the highest.**

Holy are you, and blessed is Christ Jesus,
    the bread of life.
With joy and gratitude, we remember that night
    when Jesus took a simple loaf of bread, broke it,
    and transformed it with his love, saying:
    "Take, eat, this is my body,
    the bread of life, given for you.
    Do this in remembrance of me."
After supper, Jesus took the cup,
    blessing it with gratitude
    and transforming it with love and grace, saying:
    "Drink from this, all of you.
    This is the living water, my very life,
    poured out for you and for many
    for the forgiveness of sins.
    Do this, as often as your drink it,
    in remembrance of me."

And so, in remembrance of these,
    your mighty acts of nourishing love and grace,
    we offer ourselves in praise and thanksgiving.
Called to be your people,
    and yearning to live worthy of our calling
    in the unity and peace of your Spirit,
    and in union with Christ's love for us,
    we proclaim the mystery of faith.

Christ has died.
Christ is risen.
Christ will come again.

Prayer of Consecration (Eph 4, John 6)
Pour out your Holy Spirit on us
and on these gifts of bread and wine,
that they might become for us
the bread of life and the living water.
May they strengthen us to live as your people,
and may they nourish us with grace for eternal life.
By your Spirit, make us one with you,
one in unity and peace with each other,
and one in the ministry to the world
until Christ comes in final victory
and we feast at your heavenly banquet.
Through Jesus Christ,
with the Holy Spirit in your holy Church,
all honor and glory is yours, Almighty God,
now and forevermore. Amen.

Sending Forth

Benediction (Eph 4)
In the Spirit of peace, we go into the world.
May we share the unity and love we have found here,
that others may touch the presence of Christ's peace,
and the grace of God's love.

August 8, 2021

Eleventh Sunday after Pentecost, Proper 14
B. J. Beu
Copyright © B. J. Beu

Color

Green

Scripture Readings

2 Samuel 18:5-9, 15, 31-33; Psalm 130;
Ephesians 4:25–5:2; John 6:35, 41-51

Theme Ideas

The story of Absalom's death reads like a Greek tragedy.
David is left to weep over the loss of his son. The psalmist
cries out to the Lord, noting that if God marked iniqui-
ties, none could stand. The author of Ephesians warns us
to put away falsehood and anger, which lead to sin, and
to replace evil talk and slander with acts of kindness and
with practices that build up, rather than tear down. When
Jesus describes himself as the bread of life and his hearers respond badly, he asks them not to complain among
themselves, for no one can come to him unless drawn by
God. Truly, nothing good comes from jealousy or com-
plaining, anger or resentment, plotting or scheming.

Invitation and Gathering

Centering Words (John 6)

Whoever comes to Christ will never hunger. Whoever believes in him will never thirst. Blessed be the bread of life and the living water.

Call to Worship (Ps 130)

Come, children of God.
Come and find refuge and strength.
Our souls wait for the Lord,
more than those who watch for the morning.
Come, heirs with Christ.
Come and find forgiveness and joy.
Our souls wait for the Lord,
more than those who watch for the morning.
Come, people of faith.
Come to the one who is attentive to our pleas.
Our souls wait for the Lord,
more than those who watch for the morning.

Opening Prayer (Ps 130, Eph 4, John 6)

Source of faithful love,
you redeem us from our wrongs.
We come before you today,
eager to be refreshed in body
and to be made whole in spirit.
Feed us from the living bread
that comes down from heaven,
for we are drawn to your Son
as steel is drawn to a magnet.
Build up our community of faith
through the power of your Holy Spirit,
that we may live as those
who are worthy of our calling. Amen.

Proclamation and Response

Prayer of Yearning (2 Sam 18, Ps 130, Eph 4)
Out of the depths we cry to you, O God,
with eyes streaked with tears.
For we cannot always save the ones we love,
and are left alone to taste the bitter dregs
of our sorrow.
In the lonely watches of the night,
we yearn to set aside our anger and resentment,
and embrace the paths of healing and wholeness.
In the dark night of the soul,
we long to forsake our anguish,
and embrace your mercy and compassion.
Open our hearts anew to your kindness and love,
your mercy and compassion,
that we may know in our bones
how much we are your beloved children.
Amen.

Words of Assurance (Ps 130, Eph 4)
Beloved, sorrow may last the night,
but joy comes with the morning.
Even in the midst of fear and loss,
be imitators of God as beloved children,
and live as cherished heirs with Christ.

Passing the Peace of Christ (Eph 4)
The words we say matter. Words can tear down as easily
as they can build up. Let us offer words of love and joy,
as we exchange signs of Christ's peace with one another.

Introduction to the Word (John 6:45 NRSV)
The prophets proclaim: "They shall all be taught by
God." Listen for the word of God.

Response to the Word (2 Sam 18, Eph 4)
> Do not let the sun go down on your anger,
> but be imitators of God.
> > **We will live in love, as Christ has loved us.**
> For resentment kills the spirit,
> and bitterness poisons the soul.
> > **Jealousy chokes the love in our hearts,**
> > **and scheming leads to tears.**
> Slander breaks our fellowship,
> just as arsenic poisons a well.
> > **We will not let the sun go down on our anger,**
> > **for we will be imitators of God.**
> Live in love, as Christ has lived in and through us.

Thanksgiving and Communion

Invitation to the Offering (John 6)
> Nourished by the bread of heaven and the living waters of salvation, let us return thanks to God as we collect today's offering.

Offering Prayer (Eph 4, John 6)
> Bountiful God,
> > in praise and thanksgiving for your many blessings,
> > > receive our tithes and offerings,
> > > > that they may be for the world
> > > > > signs of the bread of heaven
> > > > > > and the fullness of your grace.
> For we came here hungry for your Spirit,
> > and you fed us with food that satisfies.
> We came here thirsting for your grace,
> > and you revived us in our need.
> In humble thanks, we thank you. Amen.

Communion Prayer (John 6)
Bread of life, source of every good thing,
 we come to you this day,
  that we might never be hungry;
 we believe in you so completely,
  that we might never be thirsty.
For we are hungry for your truth,
 and thirsty for your righteousness.
Give us the bread of life
 and the cup of salvation,
  that we may never tire
   of singing your praises. Amen.

Sending Forth

Benediction (Eph 4)
Go forth from this place
and imitate the Holy One in all you do.
 **We will live with love, speak with kindness,
 touch with gentleness, walk with humbleness,
 and build up the kingdom of God.**
Go forth into the world and live in love,
as Christ has lived in and through you.

August 15, 2021

Twelfth Sunday after Pentecost, Proper 15
B. J. Beu

Color

Green

Scripture Readings

1 Kings 2:10-12; 3:3-14; Psalm 111; Ephesians 5:15-20;
John 6:51-58

Theme Ideas

Three of today's lections deal explicitly with wisdom
and the benefits of wise behavior. In 1 Kings, Solomon
inherits the throne of his father, David, and instead of
asking God for riches, success in battle, or long life,
Solomon asks God for the understanding and wisdom
needed to lead God's people. The psalmist warns that
wisdom begins with proper awe and reverence for God:
"fear of the LORD is the beginning of wisdom" (v. 10
NRSV). The epistle advocates wisdom and filling our
souls with the Holy Spirit, warning us against foolish
behavior, drunkenness, and depravity. And while the
Gospel reading does not deal explicitly with wisdom,
Jesus makes clear the wisdom of partaking of his body
and blood to attain eternal life.

Invitation and Gathering

Centering Words (Ps 111:10a NRSV)

"The fear of the LORD is the beginning of wisdom; all those who practice it have a good understanding." Let us worship in wisdom and in truth.

Call to Worship (Ps 111, Eph 5)

Let us give thanks to the Lord with all our hearts.
Great are the works of our God—
the wise take delight in them.
The works of the Lord are faithful and just.
Mighty are the precepts of our God—
the wise regard them as trustworthy and true.
The fear of the Lord is the beginning of wisdom.
Blessed are the teachings of our God—
the wise apply them in all things.
Come! Let us worship the Lord,
whose faithful love endures forever.

Opening Prayer (1 Kgs 2, Eph 5)

Eternal God, source of wisdom and understanding,
    your ways lead the upright of heart.
Give us wise and discerning minds,
        that we may seek your wisdom above earthly riches,
            as Solomon did after the death
                of his father, David.
Grant us pure and unblemished souls,
        that we may speak to one another with psalms,
            hymns, and spiritual songs.
Be with us in this time of worship,
        that we may learn to discern good from evil
            and seek to live our lives
                with your wisdom and your grace. Amen.

Proclamation and Response

Prayer of Yearning (Eph 5, John 6)
Living bread that comes down from heaven,
> we yearn to be filled with your Spirit of truth,
>> but we often embrace the folly all around us;
> we long to eat our fill of your sacred Presence,
>> but we often choose poorer fare
>>> and food that does not feed our souls;
> we desire to embrace your wisdom and your power,
>> but we often choose the path of weakness,
>>> ignoring your call to seek justice and mercy.
Come to us once more, Spirit of wisdom and truth,
> that we may abide in you, as you abide in us.
In your holy and blessed name, we pray. Amen.

Words of Assurance (John 6)
All who ask in Jesus's name, receive;
> and all who seek in the power of the Spirit, find.
Rejoice in this good news,
> and be filled with the wisdom and grace
> of our mighty God.

Passing the Peace of Christ (Eph 5)
God's faithful speak to one another with psalms, hymns, and spiritual songs. Let us greet one another with songs in our hearts and with words of blessing on our lips, as we pass the peace of Christ.

Response to the Word (1 Kgs 2, Ps 111, John 6)
Our God is the source of wisdom and understanding.
Bless us with your gifts, O God.
Our God feeds us with the bread of life
and the wellspring of our salvation.
Bless us with your grace, Christ Jesus.
Our God is the foundation of mercy and compassion.
Bless us with your gifts, Mighty Spirit.

Thanksgiving and Communion

Invitation to the Offering (Ps 111)
When the Spirit flows through us, we are people of honesty and justice. When Christ works within us, we are disciples of mercy and compassion. Let us be agents of God's overflowing grace as we collect today's offering.

Offering Prayer (Ps 111, John 6)
God of wisdom and understanding,
send these gifts into the world,
that they may become instruments of your grace;
send this offering to your people,
that it may become a source of your mercy.
May these gifts be bread and blessing
for a world in need of your mighty Spirit. Amen.

Invitation to Communion (John 6)
The bread of heaven is here, leading us into life.
We draw strength from the bread of life.
The cup of blessing is at hand, bringing us salvation.
We find life in the cup of salvation.
Eat and drink, for Christ is here, offering us eternal life.
Thanks be to God.

Communion Prayer (John 6)

Lord of life, you are the living bread
that came down from heaven.
Give us this bread,
that we may never hunger.
Source of promise, you are the cup of salvation
that was poured out for us.
Give us this cup of blessing,
that we may never thirst.
Abide in us this day,
that we may abide in you
and touch your kingdom,
which has no end. Amen.

Sending Forth

Benediction (1 Kgs 2, Ps 111, Eph 5)

Go forth and allow God's wisdom and understanding
to guide your steps.
The fear of the Lord lights our path
and illumines our path.
Go forth and let God's mercy and grace
lead your way.
The blessing of the Lord sends us forth
to be a blessing to the world.
Go with God.

August 22, 2021

Thirteenth Sunday after Pentecost, Proper 16
Karin Ellis

Color

Green

Scripture Readings

1 Kings 8:(1, 6, 10-11), 22-30, 41-43; Psalm 84;
Ephesians 6:10-20; John 6:56-69

Theme Ideas

Today we hear about God's dwelling place. In 1 Kings,
we remember the story of King Solomon bringing the
ark into the Temple. The Temple would become both a
dwelling place for God and a place of prayer for the people. The psalmist longs for a place to dwell with God, to
stand in the presence of the Lord. Turning to Ephesians
and John, we are told that Christ is the dwelling place
of God. Christ, the "Holy One of God," becomes the one
we follow. And by following Christ, by putting on the
armor of God, we are able to boldly proclaim the truth
and love of God.

Invitation and Gathering

Centering Words (Ps 84, Eph 6)

How lovely is the dwelling place of God! May our hearts become a place where God's Spirit lives. May our words become bold words of love and grace. And may our worship be worthy of the Lord.

Call to Worship (1 Kgs 8)

Welcome to this holy space
where God's Spirit dwells among us!
    We come longing to feel the presence of God.
Open your hearts, for this is a place of prayer
and healing.
    This is a place of joy and faith.
This is the place for you.
    Thanks be to God!

Opening Prayer (Eph 6, John 6)

Holy One, you have called us to this place,
    a place where we find your Spirit.
We have gathered here to pray and to be forgiven,
    to love and be loved,
        and to hear the word boldly proclaimed
            as we apply it to our lives.
Open our hearts to the mystery of your Word.
Remind us that your Word is proclaimed
    in the life of Jesus, the Christ.
Help us believe in you and in your love for us.
In the holy name of Christ we pray. Amen.

Proclamation and Response

Prayer of Confession (John 6)
Gracious God, we often forget
that you dwell in our hearts.
We fail to notice that your Holy Spirit
is present in our lives at all times.
In our forgetfulness, we stumble and fall,
we turn away from you,
we believe in worldly goods
instead of your truth.
Remind us again that you are Spirit and life;
you are all we need.
Help us turn toward your love, your healing,
and your truth.
In the name of the one who brings life,
we pray. Amen.

Words of Assurance (Ps 84:11b NRSV)
"No good thing does the LORD withhold from those who
walk uprightly." Brothers and Sisters, receive God's forgiveness and dwell in love and grace. Amen.

Passing the Peace of Christ (1 Kgs 8)
The dwelling place of God is a place for everyone.
In the name of Christ, you are welcome here.
**In the name of Christ, we come offering peace
to one another.**
I invite you to offer a hand in peace and love
to your neighbor.

Prayer of Preparation (Eph 6)
　　Abiding Spirit, may our hearts be opened
　　　　to the mystery of the gospel,
　　　　　　that the Lord of life may be made known to all.
　　Amen.

Response to the Word (1 Kgs 8, John 6)
　　Loving God, we have prayed and listened.
　　Now, may your words resonate in our hearts,
　　　　that we might come to believe you are the Holy One,
　　　　　and boldly proclaim your message of love
　　　　　　to both friend and stranger alike. Amen.

Thanksgiving and Communion

Litany (Eph 6)
　　While we are a people who believe in the resurrection,
　　there are days when challenges overwhelm us,
　　when evil forces seem to threaten all we do and say.
　　On those days, we rise:
　　　　We rise to speak truth to power.
　　We rise to live in God's righteousness
　　and in right relationship with one another.
　　　　We rise to share words of peace,
　　　　wherever our feet take us.
　　We rise to strengthen our faith in the one who loves us.
　　　　We rise to embrace the promises of God,
　　　　to protect ourselves against all hatred
　　　　and bitterness.
　　We rise to pray for one another and for ourselves.
　　　　We rise to give thanks.
　　We rise to boldly proclaim the inclusive love of Christ.
　　　　We rise because we are Easter people.

Invitation to the Offering (1 Kgs 8, John 6)

In this holy place, you are invited to bring your prayers
and your offerings before God—the one who calls us to
faith and who calls us to life.

Offering Prayer (John 6)

Gracious God, thank you for these gifts.
We offer them to you, seeking your blessing,
    that they might be used to welcome all,
        and to inspire faith in our community.
We offer our very selves,
    asking that we might become your faithful followers.
In the name of Christ, we pray. Amen.

Sending Forth

Benediction (1 Kgs 8)

Brothers and sisters, go from this place
    boldly proclaiming the love of Christ,
    so all may know the name of God.
Go in peace. Amen.

August 29, 2021

Fourteenth Sunday after Pentecost, Proper 17
B. J. Beu
Copyright © B. J. Beu

Color

Green

Scripture Readings

Song of Solomon 2:8-13; Psalm 45:1-2, 6-9; James 1:17-27;
Mark 7:1-8, 14-15, 21-23

Theme Ideas

In luscious imagery and aromatic detail, the Song of
Solomon and Psalm 45 depict the joy of union with our
loving God. Delicious fruit and oils of gladness image a
joyous world—the world as God intends. How quickly
this world descends into malicious gossip and sniping
about eating with defiled hands. The Epistle warns us
against hearing the word without living the word, and
the Gospel warns us against confusing human conven-
tion with divine instruction.

Invitation and Gathering

Centering Words (Jas 1)

Every good and perfect gift comes from above. Look to God, the creator of the heavenly lights, for a harvest of godly living.

Call to Worship (Song 2:10, Ps 45)

"Arise, my fair one, and come away," says the Lord.
We come gladly, for every good gift
comes from above.
The season of singing is upon us.
The scent of myrrh, aloe, and lavender
fills our senses.
"Arise, my fair one, and come away," calls our God.
We come to worship with joy and thanksgiving.

Opening Prayer (Song 2, Ps 45)

Bountiful God, giver of the fruit of the vine,
your call to righteous living stirs the heart
like the oils of gladness:
sweet-smelling frankincense,
sandalwood myrrh, and pungent cassia;
your charge to be doers of the word
and not hearers only, sparks the soul
like the fragrance of wild flowers
and the blossoms of spring.
Inspire true devotion in our hearts,
that we may care for your little ones
and hearken to the needs of your people.

Proclamation and Response

Prayer of Yearning (Jas 1, Mark 7)
Life-giving God, you know us better
than we know ourselves.
While we long to meet the demands of your justice,
we often settle for a touch of righteous indignation.
And though we long to resist evil
with every fiber of our being,
it is easy to confuse our anger over petty wrongs
with your anger over real misuse of power.
Teach us the difference between human precepts,
that bloom and fade like the grass,
and your life-giving ways,
that are eternal.
Help us be doers of your word, and not hearers only,
that our lives may bear the fruit of eternal life.
Amen.

Words of Assurance (Ps 45, Jas 1)
The precepts of God bring equity to the earth.
The one who anoints our lives with gladness
leads us into life and the fullness of grace.

Passing the Peace of Christ (Song 2)
The peace of Christ is sweeter than the oils of gladness.
Let us share this peace with one another as we exchange
greetings this day.

Response to the Word (Jas 1:22)
Let us be doers of the word and not hearers only.
For as we persevere in godly living,
we bear the fruit of the Spirit
and build up the whole household of God.

Thanksgiving and Communion

Invitation to the Offering (Song 2)

God calls our spirits to come away and take flight. In this season of love and light, let us be generous givers, that we may be known as children of our bountiful God.

Offering Prayer (Song 2, Jas 1)

God of light, every generous act of giving
and every perfect gift comes from you.
May the offering we bring before you this day
testify to who we are and whose we are.
And may the gifts of our hands
reflect the bounty of your harvest in our lives. Amen.

Sending Forth

Benediction (Song 2, Ps 45)

Go as God's anointed.
We go to sing songs of mirth.
Go as Christ's beloved.
We go as the family of God.
Go as gifts of the Spirit.
We go in spirit and in truth.

September 5, 2021

Fifteenth Sunday after Pentecost, Proper 18
Karin Ellis

Color

Green

Scripture Readings

Proverbs 22:1-2, 8-9, 22-23; Psalm 125;
James 2:1-10, (11-13), 14-17; Mark 7:24-37

Theme Ideas

Today's readings center on justice. Proverbs reminds us
to take care of those around us who are in need, especially the poor and vulnerable. The psalmist proclaims
the goodness of God and encourages the worshipping
community to walk in the ways of God. James shares
what it means to be faithful in the eyes of God: Faith
requires actions, specifically the actions of taking care
of those who have been forgotten by society. And in the
Gospel of Mark, a woman who has been shunned by
the community reminds Jesus that she and her daughter
are deserving of God's goodness and mercy. Jesus brings
healing to her and to many others. These passages remind
us that we too are called by God to help those around us.

Invitation and Gathering

Centering Words (Ps 125, Jas 2)

Remember God's gracious abundance and give thanks.
Remember Christ's call upon our lives to be faithful.
Open yourself to the Holy Spirit. For this is the time to
worship.

Call to Worship (Ps 125)

We gather here to worship God,
whose steadfast love endures forever.
We gather surrounded by God's Holy Spirit,
who encourages us to walk faithfully with Christ.
Praise be to God,
whose goodness and mercy fill our days.
Praise be to God,
whose ways lead to peace and justice.

Opening Prayer (Prov 22)

God of abundant life, you want the best
for your people around the globe.
You bring healing, wholeness, and new life
to all your children.
On this day, may our eyes be open
to the presence of Christ in one another.
May our ears be open to the needs of our community.
May our hands be open to serve the forgotten.
And may our hearts be open to receive your Holy Spirit
along this journey of faith.
In the name of the risen Christ, we pray. Amen.

Proclamation and Response

Prayer of Confession (Jas 2)

God of us all, your grace and mercy
    fill our lives every day.
We give you our thanks and praise.
Too often, we forget or ignore
    your presence in our lives.
Too often, we treat your children unequally,
    deeming some more important than others.
Too often, we forget that our daily actions
    need to reflect our faith.
Forgive us, and lead us to embrace abundant life
    for all of your children.
In the name of Christ, we pray. Amen.

Words of Assurance (Mark 7)

Brothers and Sisters, Christ, the great Healer,
    brings healing and wholeness to our lives.
In the name of Christ, you are forgiven.
    In the name of Christ, you are forgiven. Amen.

Passing the Peace of Christ (Jas 2)

Christ gives us the great commandment to love God
and love our neighbor. In the name of Christ, I invite
you to share peace and love with your neighbor.

Prayer of Preparation (Jas 2)

Gracious God, to proclaim your Word is a holy action.
May we be open to your Spirit at this moment,
    that we may be moved to boldly live our faith,
        each and every day. Amen.

Response to the Word (Mark 7)
> Christ's followers eagerly shared everything
> in common.
> > **May we be empowered and inspired
> > to do the same!**

Thanksgiving and Communion

Invitation to the Offering (Prov 22)
> The Lord is Creator of all and the Giver of every good
> gift. Let us offer to God a portion of these gifts, that all
> needs may be met, and that all people may come to
> know the grace and joy of God.

Offering Prayer (Prov 22)
> Gracious God, thank you for these gifts.
> We offer them to you and ask that you bless them,
> > that all may have food, clothing, and shelter.
> We also offer you our very lives,
> > asking that you bless us and use us,
> > > that all may come to know your steadfast love
> > > and your unending grace.
> In your holy name, we pray. Amen.

Sending Forth

Benediction (Ps 125, Jas 2)
> As you leave this place,
> > remember to walk in God's ways.
> Remember to dwell in the goodness of God.
> Remember to be faithful.
> May peace be upon you this day and always. Amen.

September 12, 2021

Sixteenth Sunday after Pentecost, Proper 19

B. J. Beu

Color

Green

Scripture Readings

Proverbs 1:20-33; Psalm 19; James 3:1-12; Mark 8:27-38

Theme Ideas

Proverbs, James, and Mark all agree: Willful people do
foolish and destructive things that annoy God. In Proverbs, Dame Wisdom cries out to those who love being
simple and whose actions are fraught with folly. When
calamity strikes, she will laugh, for they have been
warned. The epistle speaks of the dangers of gossip and
errant teachings, warning that an unbridled tongue can
unleash the very fires of hell. In Mark's Gospel, when
Peter rebukes Jesus for his talk of dying, Jesus rebukes
Peter for setting his mind on worldly things. Finally, the
psalmist proclaims that fear (worship) of the Lord is the
beginning of wisdom.

Invitation and Gathering

Centering Words (Prov 1)
Wisdom shouts from the streets. Above the noisy crowd
she cries out. Will we take heed and listen to her voice?

Call to Worship (Prov 1)
Wisdom shouts her warnings in the street.
We have come to forsake our foolish ways.
Wisdom longs to pour out her Spirit on all flesh.
We will not shrink from her blessings.
Wisdom imparts holy knowledge to save us.
We will not shut out the lessons she teaches.
Let us worship in spirit and in truth.

Opening Prayer (Prov 1, Ps 19, Mark 8)
Eternal God, the heavens declare your glory,
even as Wisdom proclaims your precepts
to all people.
Set our minds on the things that are above
rather than things that are below,
that when the journey becomes hard,
we may have the courage to follow you
to the bitter end.
Be with us in our hour of need,
that we may be found faithful
when Wisdom comes to call. Amen.

Proclamation and Response

Prayer of Yearning (Prov 1, Jas 3)
Wisdom of the Ages,
we yearn to forsake our foolish ways
and embrace godly knowledge.

Cry out in the streets once more,
    that we may hear your voice
        and drink deeply of your Spirit.
For we are tired of reaping the harvest of our schemes,
    and we are weary of eating the fruit of our ways.
Bridle our lips, Gracious One,
    that our tongues may speak no evil
        and utter no falsehoods,
            but rather proclaim your glory.
In your holy and righteous name, we pray. Amen.

Words of Assurance (Prov 1, Ps 19)

Following God's law is sweeter than honey,
    and far more precious than jewels.
Wisdom revives the soul and makes us whole.

Passing the Peace of Christ (Prov 1)

Holy Wisdom invites us to lives as God intends. Let us heed her invitation as we share signs of Christ's peace with one another.

Introduction to the Word (Prov 1)

Wisdom cries out in the street. In the square she shouts the ways of life. She pours her Spirit on God's faithful ones—those who give ear to her instruction and pay heed to her warnings. Listen for the word of God.

Response to the Word (Ps 19:7-8 NRSV)

"The law of the Lord is perfect, reviving the soul;
    the decrees of the Lord are sure,
    making wise the simple;
the precepts of the Lord are right, rejoicing the heart;
    the commandment of the Lord is clear,
    enlightening the eyes."

This is the word of God for the people of God.
Thanks be to God.

Thanksgiving and Communion

Invitation to the Offering (Ps 19)
Sing praises to God with the mighty firmament, for truly the heavens are telling the glory of God. As we sing our praises, let us share from our abundance, to the glory of God.

Offering Prayer (Ps 19)
Glorious God, your teachings are more to be desired
    than fine gold and precious silver;
        your blessings are more to be sought
            than all the jewels of the earth.
May the gifts we bring before you today
    share your blessings with those in need.
In Jesus's name, we pray. Amen.

Sending Forth

Benediction (Prov 1, Ps 19, Jas 3, Mark 8)
As we go forth, may the words of our mouths
be acceptable and true.
    May the meditations of our hearts
    be loving and pure.
As we leave this place, may the actions of our lives
be compassionate and just.
    May the stirrings of our hearts
    be guided by God's thoughts and wisdom.

September 19, 2021

Seventeenth Sunday after Pentecost, Proper 20
Mary Scifres
Copyright © Mary Scifres

Color

Green

Scripture Readings

Proverbs 31:10-31; Psalm 1; James 3:13–4:3, 7-8a;
Mark 9:30-37

Theme Ideas

The wisdom of servanthood guides these verses of
James, as he calls us to humility, authenticity, and
peace—three signs of the "wisdom from above." Even
the "proverbial woman" exhibits the wisdom of servanthood as she gives of herself and her gifts fully. (This
should be read as a poetic rendering of many faithful
women, not an expectation of every faithful woman.)
Perhaps it is this same wisdom that leads to the happi-
ness and fruitfulness of the first psalm. Certainly, this
wisdom of servanthood flows throughout Jesus's teachings, which must have left him a bit incredulous to hear
his disciples arguing about who was the greatest among

them. The disciples had to be reminded once more that the wisdom from above is the wisdom of serving and giving, as Jesus taught and lived.

Invitation and Gathering

Centering Words (Jas 3, Mark 9)
The wisdom from above calls to us—calling us to peace and gentleness, kindness and mercy, goodness and service.

Call to Worship (Prov 31, Jas 3, Mark 9)
Draw near to God,
and God will draw near to you.
As we come into God's presence,
the Spirit is speaking words of wisdom.
The Spirit calls us to kindness and peace.
Wisdom calls us to service and love.

Opening Prayer (Ps 1, Jas 3)
Servant God, humble our hearts and quiet our minds,
that we may reflect your servant heart
in everything we say and do.
Plant your wisdom in our lives,
that we might live your teachings
and bear fruit at just the right time.
With humble hearts, we pray. Amen.

Proclamation and Response

Prayer of Confession (Ps 1, Jas 3, Mark 9)
Servant God, humble our hearts,
even when we are proud.

Call us back to service and love,
    even when our focus is lost in the pursuit of power
        and prestige.
Remind us to be childlike in faith
    and to be faithful as your children.
Cover us with your grace
    and unify us in your peace,
        that we may embrace your wisdom from above
        and your humility from below.
In your mercy and grace, we pray. Amen.

Words of Assurance (Ps 1, Mark 9)
With the nourishment of Christ the Living Water,
    we are refreshed and made new.
In God's mercy and grace,
    we are again claimed as God's children
    and called into God's service.

Passing the Peace of Christ (Jas 3, Mark 9)
What is the wisdom from above? It is lives lived here
and now, when we are peaceful, gentle, merciful, good,
kind, fair, and genuine. Let us serve one another with
signs of this wisdom as we pass the peace of Christ.

Introduction to the Word or Response to the Word (Ps 1, Jas 3, Mark 9)
Are you wise and understanding? Know that it comes
not from hearing the word, but from embracing the
word in humility, servanthood, and love.

Thanksgiving and Communion

Offering Prayer (Jas 3, Mark 9)
God of love and service,
>we thank you for loving and serving us
>>through the grace of your Son, Christ Jesus.
Bless these gifts,
>that others may be loved and served in our giving.
Bless our lives,
>that we may love and serve one another
>>as you have loved and served us.
In your loving name, we pray. Amen.

Sending Forth

Benediction (Jas 3, Mark 9)
We go now to serve...
>**welcoming every child we meet,**
loving every person we encounter,
>**serving by all the means we can,**
in all the places we can,
>**for however long we can.**

September 26, 2021

Eighteenth Sunday after Pentecost, Proper 21
Rebecca J. Kruger Gaudino

Color

Green

Scripture Readings

Esther 7:1-6, 9-10; 9:20-22; Psalm 124; James 5:13-20; Mark 9:38-50

Theme Ideas

In Mark's Gospel, the disciples want to stop a man who heals people in Jesus's name, just because he is an outsider. Jesus challenges their exclusivist thinking and calls for the sharing of power. Then Jesus calls upon the disciples to look within their own community. How do insiders treat their own who need compassion, protection, and healing? Scholars debate the possible conflicts Jesus refers to in verses 42-47 (sexual abuse and apostasy, for example). Using hyperbole to get at the great harm insiders can do to one another, Jesus nonetheless closes with the call for those within the new Jesus community to "have salt in yourselves, and be at peace with one another" (Mark 9:50 NRSV). James fleshes out what it means to be salty and how we create a community of peace.

Invitation and Gathering

Centering Words (Jas 5, Mark 9)

> I come today, just as I am, with tears and laughter. I come to you, Jesus, Healer and Life-giver.

Call to Worship (Jas 5, Mark 9)

One: We are gathered today as a community of peace and love.

Two: Is anyone here today suffering?

All: We will pray with you.

Two: Is anyone here today rejoicing?

All: We will rejoice with you.

Two: Is anyone here today longing for healing?

All: We will anoint you with oil.

One: You are welcome to this house of peace and love.

**All: We come as we are, joyful and hurting.
We come to you, Healer, Life-giver.**

Opening Prayer (Jas 5, Mark 9)

> Jesus, Brother and Savior,
> we are grateful to find our way back to you.
> We have carried out another week's worth
> of responsibilities.
> We have watched another week's worth
> of news programs
> and have listened to another week's worth
> of predictions.
> Sometimes we have slept well;
> sometimes not.
> But here we are, before you once again,
> open to your presence.

Revive us with your love and power.
Fulfill your kingdom promises in our lives,
in our church, and in our world.
In the name of God who created us
and the Spirit who breathes new life in us,
we pray. Amen.

Proclamation and Response

Prayer of Confession (Jas 5, Mark 9)
Brother Jesus, Teacher of the Way,
we come from a busy week
of tasks and obligations.
In this quiet time,
we have a chance to reflect
on how we have lived our lives this week.
We have an opportunity to explore
the hopes that you have—
hopes for compassion for the weak,
justice for the mistreated,
and love for friends and strangers.
We thank and praise you
for your love and power.
We rejoice that you have helped us to be like you;
and we regret when we have not been like you.
Pick us up where we have fallen.
Touch us with your renewing grace, Healer on the Way.
Amen.

Words of Assurance (Jas 5)
Jesus forgives us when we wander.
He raises us up to live with courage and hope and love.
Praise be to our Brother and Savior!

Passing the Peace of Christ (Jas 5, Mark 9)

We are the gathered, much-loved, and loving community of Christ. Let us bid one another peace in Christ's name.

Response to the Word (Jas 5, Mark 9)

(Prepare several stations in your sanctuary. At each station, be prepared to accept people who come to be anointed and/or to share their joy. If you are able, have two people at each station. Use an essential oil for a blessing after people briefly share their burden. Give those who share a joy a colorful, four-inch musical note with words of joy around or within the note, such as: "Sing songs of praise" [James 5:13 NRSV]. Offer a brief prayer with those who share. For example: "As we anoint you, may the Spirit of God free you from suffering and restore you to wholeness, through Jesus the Healer"; "As we hear your joy, we praise God from whom all blessings flow!" Provide music in the background for this ritual, and close this time of ritual with a song of gratitude.)

Jesus calls us to have salt in ourselves and to be at peace with one another. One way that we show ourselves to be the flavorful, peaceful community of Jesus is by rejoicing together and bearing our burdens together. Today I invite you to come forward for anointing and prayer, so that we may walk with you, whatever your journey this week. If you long for healing, let us share your burden. If you want to share a joy, let us rejoice with you. If you wish, you may share both your burdens and your joys.

Thanksgiving and Communion

Invitation to the Offering (Jas 5, Mark 9)

Another way that we become a flavorful and peaceful community is by sharing the gifts of our lives with the world. We are a compassionate and generous people, so let us give joyfully.

Offering Prayer (Jas 5, Mark 9)

Brother Jesus, make us and our gifts salt for the world.
Make us and our gifts the source of comfort and relief
    to the suffering, joy and courage to all.
Bless our gifts of presence and treasure,
    that people may recognize you, Life-Giver,
        in our lives and in our world. Amen.

Sending Forth

Benediction (Jas 5, Mark 9)

One: Brothers and sisters, we have walked in peace with one another today.

Two: *Take this peace into your week.*

One: Brothers and sisters, we have tasted the joy of sharing our burdens and our joys.

Two: *Flavor your lives this week*
with compassion and love for others.

All: **In the name of God our Creator;**
in the peace of Jesus our Brother;
and in the power of the Spirit
go with God. Amen.

October 3, 2021

Nineteenth Sunday after Pentecost, Proper 22/
World Communion Sunday

B. J. Beu

Color

Green

Scripture Readings

Job 1:1; 2:1-10; Psalm 26; Hebrews 1:1-4; 2:5-12;
Mark 10:2-16

Theme Ideas

The readings from Job and Psalm 26 are celebrations of
faith and integrity during times of trial. God boasts of
Job's integrity, proclaiming him to be a blameless and
upright man—even after Satan had devastated his family, his livelihood, and his health. Job illustrates that suffering is no indication of whether one has lived a godly
life. The psalmist brags of personal integrity, challenging God to put this integrity to the test. Hebrews speaks
of Christ's integrity and how he was made higher than
the angels because of his faithfulness. The Gospel reading does not fit with the other texts and deals with mar-
riage, divorce, adultery, and entering the kingdom of
God like children.

Invitation and Gathering

Centering Words (Heb 1)

Christ is the light of God's glory and the imprint of God's glory. Let all God's children come to the light.

Call to Worship (Job 2, Ps 26)

Walk humbly before the Lord,
even in hardship and pain.
**We will live with integrity before God
all the days of our lives.**
Walk faithfully before our God,
even when put to the test.
**We will honor the Lord our God
all the days of our lives.**
Come! Let us worship.

Opening Prayer (Job 2, Ps 26, Heb 1, Mark 10)

Almighty God, you spoke to our ancestors long ago
through your prophets and teachers,
but today you speak to us through your Son.
In the midst of life's trials and tribulations,
help us keep our integrity
and walk faithfully in your ways.
Help us listen to the words of your Son
and become like children again,
that we may rejoice in your kingdom
and trust in your Spirit. Amen.

Proclamation and Response

Prayer of Yearning (Job 2, Ps 26)

Mysterious One, your ways can seem inscrutable.
When the road of life is smooth,
and the world is our oyster,
you seem to welcome us with open arms.
But when calamity strikes
and our need for you becomes desperate,
it feels like you slam the door between us
and we are left in the agony of silence.
We know how Jesus felt on the cross.
We also know his faith in you never waivered.
Give us the faith of Jesus,
who taught his disciples to pray to be spared
from the time of trial.
May we come to see your Presence,
whether we are receiving
the good from your hand or the bad,
for truly, you never leave us. Amen.

Words of Assurance (Heb 2)

Rejoice, for we are sanctified by God
and Jesus calls us brothers and sisters.
As Christ's sisters and brothers,
rest secure in the assurance of God's saving love.

Passing the Peace of Christ (Mark 10)

Let us have the faith and innocence of children, as we
greet our fellow children of God with signs of Christ's
peace.

Invitation to the Word (Heb 1–2)

Long ago, God spoke to our ancestors through the prophets. Today, God speaks to us through a Son, who is the very Word of God. As we listen to today's scripture, may we hear the incarnate Word of God speaking words of unfailing love.

Response to the Word (Job 2, Ps 26)

Whether life is easy at the moment or hard,
    let us continue to seek God's presence.
For in seeking, we will find.
In knocking, the door will be opened.

Thanksgiving and Communion

Offering Prayer (Heb 1)

God of love, just as you speak to us through a Son,
    speak to your world through our gifts.
May our offering receive your blessing
    and go forth to bring life and love
        to a world in need of both. Amen.

Prayer of Invitation (World Communion Sunday)

Source of unity and strength,
    in our longing for wholeness,
        we reach out to your Son,
            whose touch heals our brokenness;
    in our yearning for community,
        we take hold of the promises of Christ,
            whose life and love bind us together as one.
From lives of separation and distrust,
    knit us into one family,
        where all are welcomed and honored.

As we share the bread of life
and drink the cup of salvation,
forge us anew as one people of faith. Amen.

Sending Forth

Benediction (Job 2, Ps 26)
As you have refreshed us at your table,
weave us together as one body, one people—
a people of integrity in the midst of trials.
As you have shared your sacred meal with us,
strengthen us, that we may be united in faith—
a faith that spans the globe and the ages.
As you have blessed us with your loving presence,
send us forth in courage and peace,
rejoicing in the power of your Spirit.

October 10, 2021

Twentieth Sunday after Pentecost, Proper 23
Mary Petrina Boyd

Color

Green

Scripture Readings

Job 23:1-9, 16-17; Psalm 22:1-15; Hebrews 4:12-16; Mark 10:17-31

Theme Ideas

The life of faith often includes times of pain. In those moments, we are free to approach God honestly. We can be our true selves in God's presence and can freely express our pain, our struggles, and even our sense that God does not respond. "Where are you, my God?" the psalmist asks. Jesus understands what it is to struggle. He quoted Psalm 22:1, "My God, why have you forsaken me?" from the cross (NRSV). Hebrews proclaims Christ as our high priest, who understands the human experience of pain and mediates grace toward us. When we despair, Jesus reminds us that for God, all things are possible.

Invitation and Gathering

Centering Words (Mark 10)

It is not what we do that saves us. It is the mercy and grace of God, poured out in love. The first shall be last, for God's love turns our expectations upside down.

Call to Worship (Heb 4)

Come and worship.
God is here.
Listen for God's word.
It is alive and active.
Draw near to the source of mercy.
The God of grace is with us.

Opening Prayer (Job 23, Heb 4)

There are days, O God,
    when we feel far from your presence.
We long for you,
    yet we feel no response, no closeness.
Give us the strength to cry out in pain,
    speaking our truth.
Give us the courage to complain,
    even when there is no response.
In the emptiness,
    we long for your presence.
We wait, O God, for you.
We know that you are the source of all mercy and grace.
We trust that you will help us in times of need. Amen.

Proclamation and Response

Prayer of Confession (Job 23, Ps 22, Mark 10)
>Living God, your way can be hard.
>How can we give up everything to follow you?
>We feel so frustrated when we reach out to you
>>and feel only silence.
>We cling to what we own, fearing the future.
>Free us from our desire to accumulate more and more.
>Transform us into generous spirits,
>>sharing your gifts with the world.
>Work within us,
>>that we may know your real presence,
>>>even when we feel so little.
>We cannot do this alone.
>We need your help. Amen.

Words of Assurance (Heb 4, Mark 10)
>In Jesus, we have one who has experienced pain
>>and struggle.
>He understands us, and leads us to the one
>>who offers grace and forgiveness.
>He reminds us that all things are possible for God.

Introduction to the Word (Job 23, Heb 4)
>God's word is living and active,
>>speaking to our world today.
>It speaks powerfully to our lives.
>Trust and listen, both to words of pain and need,
>>as well as to words of mercy and grace.

Response to the Word (Mark 10)
>What must I do to inherit eternal life?
>>**Do not murder, commit adultery, steal,
>>bear false witness, defraud.**

What must I do to inherit eternal life?
Honor your father and mother.
What must I do to inherit eternal life?
Give your money to the poor and follow Jesus.
How can we do this?
It seems impossible.
Let God lead you.
In God, all things are possible.

Thanksgiving and Communion

Invitation to the Offering (Mark 10)

Jesus challenged the rich man to sell what he had and give to the poor. He challenges us today to be generous in our giving, trusting God's provision for our lives.

Offering Prayer (Mark 10)

Generous God, we bring you our gifts today.
We recognize that all we have comes from you.
May these gifts bring hope to places of pain and need.
We want to be followers of Jesus,
    who leads us from greed into service.
We offer ourselves. Amen.

Sending Forth

Benediction (Mark 10, Heb 4)

Go and follow Jesus on the pathway of love.
Share the good news of mercy and grace.
Dare to let go.
Find the courage and see what adventures
    God has in store for you.
May the blessing of the Holy One give you courage,
    for with God, nothing is impossible.

October 17, 2021

Twenty-First Sunday after Pentecost, Proper 24
Deborah Sokolove

Color

Green

Scripture Readings

Job 38:1-7, (34-41); Psalm 104:1-9, 24, 35c; Hebrews 5:1-10; Mark 10:35-45

Theme Ideas

Like Job, we complain about our misfortunes, forgetting that God is the creator and sustainer of everything that exists, ignoring that God is beyond our ability to control or even understand. Like James and John, who wanted to sit at Jesus's right and left hand when he came into his glory, we never fully comprehend God's design. When we let go of arguing with God or trying to be first in some kind of contest, we are free to take our proper place among all the wonders of God's good creation, to be grateful for all the goodness that surrounds us, and to serve one another in love.

Invitation and Gathering

Centering Words (Mark 10)

> Whoever wishes to be first among you must be the servant of all, for the Human One came not to be served but to serve.

Call to Worship (Ps 104)

> God of all creation, we come to praise and worship you.
> > **You are clothed with honor and majesty,**
> > **wrapped in light as with a garment.**
> You stretch out the heavens like a tent,
> making the clouds your chariot,
> and riding on the wings of the wind.
> > **You set the earth on its foundations,**
> > **hiding its depths with a watery cloak**
> > **that moves in the rhythm of your breath.**
> In your wisdom, you have made us in your image,
> showing us glimpses of glory in the work of your hands.
> > **God of life and love,**
> > **we come to praise and worship you.**

Opening Prayer (Job 38, Mark 10)

> God of wind and water, God of love and compassion,
> > God of all that is and all that ever shall be,
> > > when Job insisted he was innocent of every sin,
> > > you came to him in a whirlwind,
> > > > and showed him the wonders of a world
> > > > he had not made.
> When James and John asked Jesus for power and glory,
> > he told them that they would share in the bitter cup
> > that he would drink,
> > > and in the baptism of suffering
> > > that he would endure for the world.

Remind us that we are members of the body of Christ,
and that we are called to serve your creation
in love and compassion. Amen.

Proclamation and Response

Prayer of Confession (Job 38, Mark 10)
God of love and compassion,
you call us to lives of love and service,
and to share in Christ's cup of compassion
for the healing of the world.
Like Job, we complain about the unfairness of life,
seeking explanations when we don't get
everything we want.
Like James and John, we want to be first.
We want to win at the game of power and glory.
Forgive us when we forget
that we are not the center of your great creation,
and that you are the beginning and ending
of all things.

Words of Assurance (Job 38, Mark 10)
Hear the good news:
In the midst of our self-centered complaints and desires,
God opens our eyes to all that surrounds us.
In the name of Jesus Christ, you are forgiven.
In the name of Jesus Christ, you are forgiven.
Glory to God. Amen.

Passing the Peace of Christ (Job 38, Mark 10)
Jesus came not to be served but to serve, so let us serve
one another with signs of peace.

The peace of Christ be with you.
The peace of Christ be with you always.

Prayer of Preparation (Job 38, Mark 10)
God of all creation,
you laid the foundation of the earth
while all the morning stars sang together,
and all the heavenly beings shouted for joy.
You created us in your image,
to love and serve one another
as Jesus loved and served his friends.
As we listen to your deeds of old,
open our hearts and minds
to hear the voice of your Holy Spirit. Amen.

Response to the Word (Job 38)
God of all creation, like Job before us,
we have heard your voice in the whirlwind,
and remember that you are the center of our lives.

Thanksgiving and Communion

Offering Prayer (Job 38)
Creator of all that is and all that ever shall be,
we offer you these gifts in gratitude
for placing us in a world
filled with wonder and beauty. Amen.

Great Thanksgiving
Christ be with you.
And also with you.
Lift up your hearts.
We lift them up to God.

Let us give our thanks to the Holy One.
It is right to give our thanks and praise.

It is a right, good, and a joyful thing,
always and everywhere to give our thanks to you.
You fill the sky with clouds and rain,
and rattle the earth with the sound of thunder.
You cover the land with green plants
and flowering shrubs,
with fruit trees and grain,
and with all that we need to nourish our bodies.
You give us wisdom and understanding,
and show us the wonders of the universe.

And so, with your creatures on earth
and all the heavenly chorus,
we praise your name and join their unending hymn:
Holy, holy, holy Lord, God of power and might,
heaven and earth are full of your glory.
Hosanna in the highest. Blessed is the one
who comes in the name of the Lord.
Hosanna in the highest.

Holy are you, and holy is your child, Jesus Christ,
who reminded his disciples
that they were not the center of the universe,
and just as he had come not to be served
but to serve, so they, too, should love
and serve one another.

On the night in which he gave himself up,
Jesus took bread, broke it, saying:
"Take, eat, all of you.
This is my body, broken for you.
Whenever you eat it,
do so in remembrance of me."

After supper, he took the cup, saying:
"This is the cup of the new covenant,
poured out for the healing of the world.
Whenever you drink it,
do so in remembrance of me."

And so, in remembrance of your mighty acts
in Jesus Christ, we proclaim the mystery of faith.
Christ has died.
Christ is risen.
Christ will come again.

Pour out your Holy Spirit on us,
and on these gifts of bread and wine.
Make them be for us the body and blood of Christ,
that we may be united with Christ forever
in the power of the Holy Spirit.
Amen.

Sending Forth

Benediction (Job 38, Mark 10)
Just as Jesus came not to be served but to serve
and to give his life for the sake of the world,
let us go forth to love and serve all of creation
in the name of the one who calls us
to delight in all its goodness.
Amen.

October 24, 2021

Twenty-Second Sunday after Pentecost, Proper 25

B. J. Beu
Copyright © B. J. Beu

Color

Green

Scripture Readings

Job 42:1-6, 10-17; Psalm 34:1-8, (19-22); Hebrews 7:23-28; Mark 10:46-52

Theme Ideas

Job and Psalm 34 present problems for preachers and worship leaders alike. While the psalmist insists that God spares and protects the righteous, Job is a chilling example of the devastation that God can bring upon anyone. The author paints Job's vindication and the restoration of Job's fortunes as of greater value than what Job lost in God's test of his faithfulness. But can anything remotely make up for the loss of one's family—much less to such a test of faith? If these texts are used, they must not be sugarcoated; their full cognitive dissonance must be allowed to play out—for such is the experience of real life. The Gospel reading adds a wonderful avenue for reflection. Blind Bartimaeus is offered the brass ring—Jesus offers him anything he asks for. Not surprisingly, Bartimaeus asks for the return of his physical sight. What would Job or we ask for: our children back, our physical sight returned? Or would we ask to see with God's eyes or to have God's salvation? What do we seek, and how well do we really see?

Invitation and Gathering

Centering Words (Ps 34)

Taste and see that the Lord is good. God's steadfast love endures forever.

Call to Worship (Job 42, Ps 34)

Magnify the Lord. Exalt God's holy name.
How can we praise God amidst so much suffering?
God is Lord over all—both good and evil.
Only the saints can comprehend such things.
The Lord hears the pleas of the perishing,
and transforms the suffering of the faithful
into a deeper joy.
Restore our fortunes, O God,
when calamity strikes.
Magnify the Lord, you righteous of the Lord.
We will exalt God's holy name.

Opening Prayer (Job 42, Mark 10)

God our healer, source of everlasting mercy,
give us the courage to cry out in our need
when the crowd seeks to silence us,
as did blind Bartimaeus outside Jericho;

give us the wisdom to admit our limitations
    and accept our limited understanding,
        as did Job before us;
give us the confidence to sing your praises
    in the midst of fear and doubt,
        as the psalmist did in David's court.
Grant us your healing balm, O God,
    that we may be truly made well and whole
        and follow you all the days of our lives. Amen.

Proclamation and Response

Prayer of Yearning (Job 42, Ps 34, Mark 10)

God of mystery and blessing,
    we long to be counted among the wise,
        and not among the foolish
            who speak without knowledge;
    we yearn to be found among the righteous,
        and not among those who boast without cause;
    we desire to be sincere agents of your grace,
        and not be as those who speak empty words
            without true compassion.
Give us eyes to truly see
    when we only see what others have,
        and not what they have lost.
Give us hearts of flesh
    when we are absorbed in our own desires,
        and ignore the needs of others.
As blind Bartimaeus before us,
    grant us the courage to cry out our need,
        for you are ever drawing near. Amen.

Words of Assurance (Heb 7)

Christ intercedes for us, and saves everyone
who comes to God in his name.
Draw near to God through Christ,
and God will draw near to you.

Passing the Peace of Christ (Mark 10)

Even when the crowds shout for us to be silent, Jesus beckons us to him, that we might be healed. Let us give thanks for the mercies of God as we exchange signs of Christ's peace with one another.

Response to the Word (Mark 10)

Pay no heed to the crowd
or to those who would silence your call to Christ.
Shout out your needs
and the deepest desires of your heart,
for Christ came to save us.
Make Christ the center of your life
and you will be made whole.

Call to Prayer (Ps 34)

Seek the Lord, and God will answer. Happy are those who take refuge in our God. The Lord will deliver them from their tears. Let us pray.

Thanksgiving and Communion

Offering Prayer (Job 42, Ps 34, Mark 10)

Mighty God, just as you restore sight to the blind
and benevolence to the afflicted,
use these offerings to provide refuge for the lost
and mercy for those who suffer.

May our gifts find those who cry out in their need
and who seek you with their whole hearts.
We ask this in Jesus's name,
the name above all names. Amen.

Sending Forth

Benediction (Ps 26, Heb 7)
We once were broken, but now are whole.
We go with peace in our hearts.
We once were blind, but now we see.
We go with hope for our lives.
We once were lost, but now are found.
We go with joy and thanksgiving.
We once were alone, but now are family.
We go with God.

October 31, 2021

Twenty-Third Sunday after Pentecost, Proper 26/Reformation Sunday

Mary Scifres

Color

Green

Scripture Readings

Ruth 1:1-18; Psalm 146; Hebrews 9:11-14; Mark 12:28-34

Theme Ideas

Love. Love God, love self, love neighbor. The gospel in a word is *love*! Jesus and the scribe agree in today's Gospel lesson: the central tenet of faith is love. The foreigner Ruth, recently widowed, knows this instinctively when she follows her loving heart and travels with her mother-in-law to a land she has never known. This love-connection may be taken lightly on reality television, but not so in our scriptures. The call to love demands courage and strength, sacrifice and servanthood. The call to love is God's call to all who would follow Christ.

Invitation and Gathering

Centering Words
♫ "Love…love…love…love, the gospel in a word is love. Love your neighbor as your brother, love…love…love." Everything we need to know is taught in a Sunday school song.
(B. J. Beu)

Call to Worship (Ruth 1, Mark 12)
Come into the land of God.
We come seeking the land of love.
Live as the people of Christ.
We gather to grow as a community of love.
Follow in the ways of the Lord.
We move forward on the path of love.
Come, young and old, friend and foreigner,
for all are welcome here.
We come to live and grow in the love of Christ.
Praise God for this wonderful gift!

–Or–

Call to Worship (Ps 146)
Praise the God of love.
We rejoice in this abundant love.
Praise the God of hope.
We sing praise for this life-giving hope.
Praise the God of new beginnings.
We give thanks for this chance at new life.

Opening Prayer (Ruth 1, Mark 12)
O God, you are our God,
and we come as your people on earth.

Gather us in,
that we may remember the ties
that bind us together in your love.
Write your law upon our hearts,
that others may find us to be
generous and loving friends.
Strengthen us by your Spirit,
that we may live in love—
a love that transforms our lives,
even as we help to transform
the lives of others.
In the hope of your miraculous love, we pray. Amen.

Proclamation and Response

Prayer of Confession (Ruth 1, Ps 146, Mark 12)
Helper God,
be the hope that overcomes our despair;
be the love that overcomes our hatred;
be the mercy that overcomes our sin.
Set us free from the prisons of our own making,
and release us from the bonds that bind us.
Forgive us and watch over us.
Welcome us home
into the loving arms of your mercy.
In Christ's name, we pray. Amen.

Words of Assurance (Mark 12)
You are not far from the kingdom of God,
for in Christ we are given grace and forgiveness.
Praise God for this marvelous gift!

Passing the Peace of Christ (Ruth 1, Mark 12)

As the church, we gather together in the spirit of Ruth and Naomi. Where you go, I will go. Where you dwell, I will dwell. Your God will be my God, and your people will be my people. We are bound as one body in love of God, neighbor, and self. Let us share this message of unity as we exchange signs of peace and love.

Response to the Word (Mark 12)

Love God with all your heart
and mind and soul and strength.
We love as God loves us.
Love your neighbors as yourself,
with kindness and care.
We love as God loves us.
Love yourself with gentleness,
with mercy and grace.
We love as God loves us.

Thanksgiving and Communion

Invitation to the Offering (Ps 146)

As the people of God, we are called to be justice for the oppressed, food for the hungry, freedom for the imprisoned, and sight for the blind. Let us lift up those in need, as we share gifts for the church's mission.

Offering Prayer (Ps 146, Mark 12)

God of justice and love,
transform these offerings,
that they may be gifts of justice and love
for a world in need of hope and help.
Let love flow through these offerings,
that they may become gifts of love for the world.

Sending Forth

Benediction (Ruth 1, Mark 12)
Go to love God and neighbor.
We go forth in the love of God.
Go to welcome the stranger.
We go forth with love for the world.

November 1, 2021

All Saints Day
Deborah Sokolove

Color

White

Scripture Readings

Isaiah 25:6-9; Psalm 24; Revelation 21:1-6a; John 11:32-44

Theme Ideas

The true home of God is among humans. In the realm of God, all that is broken will be healed, and all will live in peace, joy, and eternal life.

Invitation and Gathering

Centering Words (Ps 24)
The earth and all that is in it belongs to the Holy One. Look, this is our God, for whom we have waited. Who will come to the hill of the Holy One and seek the face of God?

Call to Worship (Isa 25, Ps 24)
The earth and all that is in it belongs to the Holy One.
Look, here is our God,
for whom we have waited.

This is the Holy One, for whom we have waited.
Let us be glad and rejoice in our salvation.
Who shall ascend the hill of the Holy One?
And who shall stand in this holy place?
We come, seeking the face of God.

Opening Prayer (Ps 24, Rev 21)
Faithful Redeemer,
 you are the beginning and end of all things.
You promise to wipe away every tear,
 that death and mourning will be no more.
You make your home among us,
 and abide with us as our God.
Teach us to live like the saints you call us to be,
 that we may truly be your people,
  living and doing your will,
   in the name of Jesus, who is the Christ.
Amen.

Proclamation and Response

Prayer of Confession (Ps 24, Rev 21, John 11)
Patient, Forgiving Spirit, we come seeking your face.
 We hold on to ancient angers and hurts,
  and refuse to believe that you alone
   can make all things new.
Like Mary and Martha,
 we have forgotten your promise of eternal life.
 Like the crowd that mourned for Lazarus,
  we could not believe we would see your glory.
Forgive our unbelief, O God.
 Bring us back, and restore our trust in you.

Words of Assurance (Rev 21)

The Holy One shows us a vision
of a new heaven and a new earth,
where everyone will live in peace and blessing.
Trusting in God's promise to wipe away all our tears,
in the name of Christ, you are forgiven.
In the name of Christ, you are forgiven.
Glory to God. Amen.

Passing the Peace of Christ

Rejoicing in the love of the one for whom we wait, let us
exchange signs of Christ's peace.
May the peace of Christ be with you,
today and always.
May the peace of Christ be with you,
today and always.

Invitation to the Word (Ps 24)

Listen to the Holy One, for whom we have waited.
We rejoice in the words of our salvation.

Response to the Word (Rev 21, John 11)

Alpha and Omega, the beginning and ending of all creation, in your word we are unbound from death, and brought out into eternal life in you.
Amen.

Thanksgiving and Communion

Offering Prayer (Isa 25, Rev 21)

God of abundance,
you offer us rich food and fine wines;
you bless us with all the bounty
of your heavenly banquet.

May the gifts we offer this day,
    provide food and drink to those who go without,
        that all may come to know
            the blessings of your table
                in this world and in the world to come.
(B. J. Beu)

Communion Prayer (Isa 25, Rev 21)

Generous Giver of all that we need,
    accept these simple gifts of bread and wine,
        that we may one day share in your holy feast
            spread out through all the world.
We pray in the name of Jesus, your holy child,
    who sets the table for all people—
        a table of rich food and abundant joy.
        Amen.

Great Thanksgiving

Christ be with you.
    And also with you.
Lift up your hearts.
    We lift them up to God.
Let us give our thanks to the Holy One.
    It is right to give our thanks and praise.

It is a right, good, and a joyful thing
    always and everywhere to give our thanks to you,
    Alpha and Omega, beginning and ending
    of all creation.
In the days of Isaiah, you promised to lead
    all the nations to your holy mountain
    and swallow up death forever.

You have revealed the coming of a new heaven
    and new earth, in which every tear
    will be wiped from our eyes,
    and all will feast at your heavenly banquet.

And so, with your saints now on earth
    and all the company of heaven,
    we praise your name
    and join their unending hymn, saying:
    Holy, holy, holy One, God of power and might,
        Heaven and earth are full of your glory.
    Hosanna in the highest. Blessed is the one
        who comes in your holy name.
    Hosanna in the highest.

Holy are you, and holy is your child, Jesus Christ.
When he raised Lazarus from the grave,
    he showed us all your glory,
    giving thanks only to you and praising your name.

On the night in which he gave himself up,
    Jesus took bread, broke it, saying:
    "Take, eat, all of you.
    This is my body, broken for you.
    Whenever you eat it,
    do so in remembrance of me."
After supper, he took the cup, saying:
    "This is the cup of the new covenant,
    poured out for the healing of the world.
    Whenever you drink it,
    do so in remembrance of me."

And so, in remembrance of your mighty acts
in Jesus Christ, we proclaim the mystery of faith.
>   **Christ has died.**
>   **Christ has risen.**
>   **Christ will come again.**

Pour out your Holy Spirit on us
>   and on these gifts of bread and wine.
Make them be for us the body and blood of Christ,
>   so that we may become one with Christ,
>   one with each other,
>   and one in ministry to all the world,
>   until all things are made new.
Alpha and Omega, Beginning and End,
>   Spirit of new beginnings,
>   we praise your holy, eternal, triune name.
>   **Amen.**

Sending Forth

Benediction (Ps 24, Rev 21)
>   Go into the world as the living body of Christ,
>   bringing eternal life to all who seek God's face.
>   **Amen.**

November 7, 2021

Twenty-Fourth Sunday after Pentecost, Proper 27

Karen Clark Ristine

Color

Green

Scripture Readings

Ruth 3:1-5; 4:13-17; Psalm 127; Hebrews 9:24-28; Mark 12:38-44

Theme Ideas

Caring for others and caring for oneself are themes in today's scriptures. Boaz cares for his kin, Ruth. A community cares for the earthly ancestors of Christ by caring for the infant Obed. The psalmist warns against worry, saying anxiety is needless and advocating self-care. Christ cares for all in the epistle text. And the Gospel includes the classic admonition to love neighbor as yourself. Regardless of which text is featured, caring can be a central focus.

Invitation and Gathering

Centering Words (Ps 127)

Care for us Holy One,
    and help us see the goodness
        of your caring presence in our lives.
Help us welcome you into our homes.
Help us release toil and anxiety and find peace.

Call to Worship (Mark 12)

Love the Lord your God.
    We love with all our heart.
Love the Lord your God.
    We love with all our soul.
Love the Lord your God.
    We love with all our mind.
Love the Lord your God.
    We love with all our strength.

Opening Prayer (Heb 9, Mark 12)

Abiding and caring God,
    help us remember that you are present with us,
        calling us to be our best selves.
Help us learn to love ourselves,
    that we might learn to love our neighbors.
With the caring example of Christ,
    we seek to be your love and care in the world.
Amen.

Proclamation and Response

Prayer of Confession (Mark 12)
O God, we have not invested all that we are—
our hearts, minds, soul, and strength—
in loving you.
And each day,
we struggle to love one another to the fullest.
Receive our heartfelt confession,
and hear our gratitude
for your grace and forgiveness. Amen.

Words of Assurance
In the name of Jesus Christ, you are forgiven.
In the name of Jesus Christ, you are forgiven.

Response to the Word (Ruth 3, Mark 12)
We will care as Boaz cared for Ruth.
We will care as Naomi cared for the ancestors of Christ.
We will care as Jesus taught us to care
for our neighbors and ourselves.

Thanksgiving and Communion

Offering Prayer (Ruth 3, Ps 127)
Help us give ourselves with abandon to one another
as Naomi and Ruth gave themselves to each other.
Help us give ourselves without anxiety in service.
Help us give in ways that help this congregation
mend lives through love.
May these gifts heal an aching world
and care for all creation. Amen.

Invitation to Communion
    Come to this feast of love.
    Come to this blessing table.
    Come and know love.

Sending Forth

Benediction (Mark 12)
    Go out in love to care for strangers.
    Go out in love to care for kin.
    Go out in love to care for neighbors.
    Go out in love to care for yourselves, beloved of God.
    Amen.

November 14, 2021

Twenty-Fifth Sunday after Pentecost, Proper 28
Karin Ellis

Color

Green

Scripture Readings

1 Samuel 1:4-20; 1 Samuel 2:1-10 (or Psalm 16); Hebrews 10:11-14, (15-18), 19-25; Mark 13:1-8

Theme Ideas

A priestly theme runs though today's lessons. We first hear the story of Hannah, a faithful woman who went to the Temple to pray for a child. If she found favor with God, she promised to dedicate her son to the Lord's work, which she did. The psalmist echoes the words of the faithful, rejoicing in all God has done. The writer of Hebrews confesses that Christ is our priest, making the ultimate sacrifice for us and calling us together to love and do good deeds. And Mark recounts Jesus's foretelling of the end times, when not even the stone buildings will be left standing. Jesus will bring forth a new kind of kingdom, but it will not be easy. These readings beg the question, "How might we be faithful?"

Invitation and Gathering

Centering Words (Ps 16)

In the presence of God, we find the fullness of joy. May this time of worship be full of joy, surprises, healing, and love.

Call to Worship (1 Sam 1, 2; Ps 16; Heb 10)

Christ is waiting here for us.
To welcome us.
To show you the path of life.
To love us.
To hear our prayers.
To be present with us always.
Come and worship.
We are here to praise the Lord!

Opening Prayer (1 Sam 1, 2; Heb 10)

Creating God, we give you thanks for this day,
    for the breath of life in our bodies,
        and for the ability to gather here
            as your faithful followers.
During this time,
    may our prayers be honest and heart-felt.
May we support and encourage one another.
May our words be kind and compassionate.
May we be inspired by your Holy Spirit
    to do good deeds,
        and to love without question or boundaries.
And may we glorify you with our whole being.
In the name of Christ, we pray. Amen.

Proclamation and Response

Prayer of Confession (1 Sam 1, 2; Mark 13)
>Almighty God, the road of the faithful is hard
>>and filled with challenges.
>Sometimes we complain.
>Sometimes we take a different road.
>Sometimes we allow others to lead us astray.
>Sometimes we forget to follow your Son, Jesus.
>Forgive us.
>Help us meet whatever challenges we face.
>Help us rise when we fall.
>Help us turn toward you,
>>our Savior and Redeemer.
>In the name of the one who loves us unconditionally,
>>we pray. Amen.

Words of Assurance (Heb 10:17)
>"I will remember their sins no more," says the Lord.
>Brothers and Sisters, your sins are forgiven
>>and you are given a new chance
>>to walk in the ways of Christ.
>Thanks be to God! Amen.

Passing the Peace of Christ (Ps 16)
>My heart is glad,
>>**and my spirit rejoices!**
>In thanksgiving and praise,
>>**let us offer one another signs of peace.**

Prayer of Preparation (1 Sam 1, 2)
>Loving God, we are here to pour out our hearts
>>before you.

Fill up our hearts with your word,
>   that we might strengthen our faith
>   and deepen our love for you. Amen.

Response to the Word (Mark 13)

The disciples wondered when the kingdom of God
would become a reality.
>   **The time is now.**
It will not be easy.
>   **We are strong and ready to bring forth new life
>   and renewed hope for the future.**
May it be so!

Thanksgiving and Communion

Invitation to the Offering (1 Sam 1, 2; Mark 13)

Hannah went to the temple and offered her prayers to
God. Jesus offered his love and his life. May this be the
time when we offer our gifts to God in thanksgiving for
God's abiding presence in our lives.

Offering Prayer (Ps 16, Heb 10)

Lord of life and love, we offer these gifts to you.
Bless them and use them,
>   that others might be encouraged in the faith.
Gracious God, use our lives as well.
Help us share your story
>   and pour out your love on everyone we meet.
In the name of Christ, we pray. Amen.

Sending Forth

Benediction (Heb 10, Mark 13)
People of God, be encouraged, be hopeful, be faithful.
Know that Christ is the Lord of our lives,
the one who shares extravagant love.
Go and do likewise.
Go in peace. Amen.

November 21, 2021

Twenty-Sixth Sunday after Pentecost, Proper 29/ Christ the King/Reign of Christ Sunday
James Dollins

Color

White

Scripture Readings

2 Samuel 23:1-7; Psalm 132:1-12, (13-18);
Revelation 1:4b-8; John 18:33-37

Theme Ideas

In the beautiful hymn "How Can I Keep from Singing," the refrain proclaims: "Since love is Lord of heaven and earth, how can I keep from singing?" Reign of Christ Sunday heralds the end of the Christian year with this same proclamation: God's love in Christ Jesus reigns above every other power. Our scriptures from 2 Samuel and Psalm 132 foresee this coming Messiah, as our text from Revelation celebrates Christ's eternal reign. May Love reign in our own hearts above every other motivation—be it fear, sadness, or anything that would separate us from God and from one another.

Invitation and Gathering

Centering Words (John 18, Rev 1)

Come, rest from your struggles, your worries, and your work. May the Lord of Love reign above every earthly power, and in our hearts as well.

Call to Worship (Rev 1:8 NRSV)

Grace to you and peace from the one who is, who was, and who is to come.

**Grace from Jesus, the faithful witness
and lover of our souls.**

"I am the Alpha and the Omega," says the Lord, "who is and who was and who is to come."

**To the one who loves us
and who freed us from our sins,
to God be the glory and power forever and ever.
Amen.**

Opening Prayer (John 18:37c NRSV)

Lord of Love, we give thanks
that we belong to your kingdom,
which is higher and greater
than any human power.
Every child and elder, every neighbor and foreigner
finds a home in your kingdom of peace.
Jesus said, "Everyone who belongs to the truth
listens to my voice."
Give us ears to hear the voice of Christ our king
above the din of human voices.
Settle the dust that becomes stirred up inside us
by debate or division.

Give us eyes to see your will
and ears to hear your word,
so that we may love one another,
love ourselves,
and love you with all that we are.
In your holy name, we pray. Amen.

Proclamation and Response

Prayer of Confession (John 18, Rev 1)
God of Grace, we feel threatened by forces
that seem greater than ourselves.
As Pontius Pilate taunted Jesus,
daring him to spar over earthly power,
we are tempted to lower ourselves
to compete and compare with one another.
Forgive us when we forget that we belong, above all,
to your way and your truth.
When we feel inclined to fight or flee,
let us instead seek refuge
in your wisdom and your grace.
Guide us not to react badly,
but to respond faithfully.
Inspire us to answer insult with creative acts of love.
Let us trust not in our own power,
but in the strength of your love,
which reigns in the heavens
and on the earth forevermore. Amen.

Words of Assurance (Rev 1:8 NRSV)
"I am the Alpha and the Omega," says the Lord,
the one who loves you and frees you from your sin.
In the name of Jesus Christ, we are forgiven!
Amen.

Response to the Word (Matt 6 KJV, Adapted)
Inspire us, dear Christ, to love every neighbor,
whether friend or enemy.
Your kingdom come on earth as it is in heaven.
Let your church become a powerful force for good.
Your will be done on earth as it is in heaven.
Help us feed every neighbor who is hungry
and feels abandoned.
Give us this day our daily bread.
Cast out all evil, injustice, and oppression.
Forgive us our trespasses,
and deliver us from evil.
Jesus, remember us when you come into your kingdom.
Your kingdom come on earth as it is in heaven.
Amen.

Thanksgiving and Communion

Offering Prayer (Ps 132, John 18)
Spirit of Life and Love, reign in us today.
Use these gifts, the fruit of our labor,
to make your church
an instrument of peace for the world.
May we not rest until your peaceable kingdom
reigns in every heart.
Move us this day to feed the hungry, befriend the lonely,
protect the afflicted, and proclaim Christ's love
to all your creation.
In your holy name, we pray. Amen.

Sending Forth

Benediction (John 18)
We are all citizens of Christ's peaceable kingdom.
Go and tell others that they too belong to God. Amen.

November 25, 2021

Thanksgiving Day

Rebecca J. Kruger Gaudino, Mary Scifres, and B. J. Beu

Copyright © B. J. Beu and Mary Scifres

Color

Red

Scripture Readings

Joel 2:21-27; Psalm 126; 1 Timothy 2:1-7; Matthew 6:25-33

Theme Ideas

Our readings hold together two experiences in life that seem at odds with one another: the experience of human need and sorrow, and the experience of God's lavish love and care. Speaking to a famine-struck people, the prophet Joel contends that God's ordained rhythms of creation will re-establish themselves in abundance. To "those who sow in tears," the psalmist tells stories of God's goodness, and then promises sheaves of joy. The writer of 1 Timothy holds forth a vision of unity, where all people are reconciled to God. In Matthew, Jesus invites those who are oppressed by worry to imagine life as a bird or a lily—worry-free and reliant on God's care alone. These readings do not deny sorrow, need, loss, and anxiety. Instead, they invite us to remember God's provision in the past, and to expect God to provide for us today.

Invitation and Gathering

Centering Words (Ps 126)

Let those who sow in tears, bear sheaves of joy this Thanksgiving. Let those who have endured a long winter of waiting, sing for joy at the rich harvest of God's bountiful love.

(B. J. Beu)

Call to Worship (Joel 2, Ps 126)

Be glad and rejoice in the Lord our God.

God has blessed us with abundant rain.

The trees bear their fruit.

The threshing floors are full of grain.

The vats overflow with wine and oil.

We will eat in plenty and be satisfied.

The earth provides all we need to live.

God has done great things for us.

Be glad and rejoice in the Lord our God.

–Or–

Call to Worship (Joel 2, Ps 126, Matt 6)

Those who go out weeping,

shall come home with shouts of joy!

Those who worry about their life,

shall learn that God knows all their needs.

Those who have experienced the swarming locust,
shall eat in plenty and be satisfied.
Those who long for comfort,
shall be glad and rejoice,
for God has done great things!

Opening Prayer (Joel 2, Ps 126, Matt 6, 1 Tim 2)
Maker of heaven and earth,
you enliven your creation:
causing the skies to rain,
the soil to be rich and fertile,
the fields to yield abundant crops,
and the trees to bear fruit.
Enliven us once more, Holy One.
Call us forth into the joy of your harvest:
from tears to shouts of joy,
from calamity to plenty,
from worry to faith,
and from what is false to what is true.
You are our God,
there is no other.
We praise your name,
for you have dealt wondrously with us
and will do so again. Amen.

Proclamation and Response

Prayer of Yearning (Joel 2, Ps 126, 1 Tim 2, Matt 6)
We gather before you today, O God,
intent on giving you thanks.
We remember the wonders of your past,
even as we yearn for the wonders
you have in store for us.

We long to touch your mercy and your care,
    for our lives are often sown with tears.
Help our rulers and authorities
    seek to the building of your kingdom
        and the triumph of your righteousness.
Restore our fortunes, O God,
    like streams watering the wilderness,
        that we may reap with shouts of joy
            what was planted in sorrow. Amen.

Words of Assurance (Ps 126, Matt 6)

Through Christ, God's love has done great things for us.
Through Christ, God's grace restores our life
    and makes us whole once more.
(Mary Scifres)

Passing the Peace of Christ (1 Tim 2, Matt 6)

Share with one another signs of peace and love. Show Christ to one another, that we may be reminded of the peace that passes all understanding.
(Mary Scifres)

Response to the Word (Matt 6, Joel 2)

Look at the birds of the air.
    They fly free of our worries:
    no fields to weed and harvest,
    no barns to fill.
And yet God feeds them.
Consider the lilies of the field.
    They grow free of our worries:
    no clothing to buy, no shoes to match.
And yet God clothes them in splendor.

So do not worry. Do not fear.
God knows our needs.
We will eat in plenty!
We will be satisfied!
Rejoice! God looks after our needs.

Thanksgiving and Communion

Invitation to the Offering (Joel 2)

Be glad and rejoice! Just as summer brought green forests and sunny days, so now fall brings abundant fields and changing leaves. As the rain falls upon us, may we remember that the seasons, the fertile earth, and the blessings they yield, are gifts from God—gifts to be shared with those in need.
(Mary Scifres)

Offering Prayer

Gracious God, source of every blessing,
we look forward to your harvest each year.
Our tables overflow with the bounty of this good earth,
but our tables pale in comparison
to the splendor that awaits us,
and all of your children,
at your heavenly banquet.
Receive these offerings,
as we thank you for your many blessings,
and help us be mindful of those who go without,
as we feast and make merry
during this festive season. Amen.
(B. J. Beu)

Sending Forth

Benediction (Ps 126, Matt 6)

Go home with hearts filled with hope!
For God, who has restored us in the past,
will do so again.
Let us go home singing songs of hope!
Go home with shouts of joy!
For God, who knows our tears,
will not leave us comfortless.
Let us go home singing songs of joy!
Go home with souls touched by grace!
For God, who knows our needs and daily cares,
will provide us with the blessings of life.
Let us go home singing songs of grace and mercy!

November 28, 2021

First Sunday of Advent

B. J. Beu

Color

Purple

Scripture Readings

Jeremiah 33:14-16; Psalm 25:1-10; 1 Thessalonians 3:9-13; Luke 21:25-36

Theme Ideas

The promised one of God is coming. Jeremiah foretold of a "righteous Branch" that would spring up for David. Luke speaks of Jesus as the Son of Man who is coming in clouds of glory. Whatever title we use, God's promised one will execute justice and bring salvation to God's people. Be alert, therefore, for redemption draws near.

Invitation and Gathering

Centering Words (Jer 33, Ps 25)

A righteous branch has sprung forth to bring goodness and justice to our world.

Call to Worship (Jer 33, Ps 25)
Our promised salvation is at hand.
A righteous branch has sprung forth,
bringing hope to our world.
Our eyes have beheld the goodness and mercy
of the Lord.
A Son has been given to us,
bringing justice and virtue to our land.
Our hearts have felt the stirrings of God's Presence.
The Spirit of truth is here to heal us,
teaching transgressors God's ways.
Let us worship the God of our salvation.

Opening Prayer (Ps 25, Luke 21)
Righteous One, your glory shines brighter than the sun.
We remember your compassion and your faithful love,
as we come to worship this day.
Lift up our souls to meet the challenges we face,
as we seek to bear the fruit of your salvation.
May your righteous branch grow within our hearts,
that our lives may abound in mercy
and steadfast love.
And may we be found ready and waiting
when the one drawing near
comes with power and glory
to bring us to you. Amen.

Proclamation and Response

Prayer of Yearning (Jer 33, Luke 21)
Almighty God, your promises of old strengthen us
during these dark times.

We yearn to learn to read the signs of your coming:
in the sun, moon, and stars;
in the roaring of the seas and the waves;
and in the tumult of our world.
Yet, we have seen it all before
and nothing seems to change.
We long to live with courage
in an age where wars are fought for peace
and freedoms are stripped in the name of liberty.
Grant us the wisdom that comes from waiting,
and teach us the patience that leads to godliness
as our savior draws near. Amen.

Words of Assurance (Jer 33, Ps 25, Luke 21)

We worship a God of mercy,
who abounds in steadfast love.
The one who is God's righteous branch
draws near to save us from our weakness,
and to seal us in God's love.

Passing the Peace of Christ (Jer 33)

The Lord is our righteous branch, the gateway to everlasting life. In celebration of this mighty gift, let us share signs of peace with one another this day.

Introduction to the Word (Ps 25)

Make your ways known, O Lord,
in the reading of today's scriptures.
Teach us your paths,
and open the gates of understanding.
Lead us into your truth,
and instruct our hearts,
for you are the God of our salvation.

Response to the Word (Jer 33, Luke 21)

In this season of Advent, O God,
> teach us to read the signs of the times,
> > and help us wait patiently
> > > for the coming of your Son.

For he is our righteous branch,
> and we need his justice and mercy
> > to meet the challenges and adversities
> > > in our world. Amen.

Thanksgiving and Communion

Invitation to the Offering (Ps 25)

Those who keep God's covenant and decrees walk in the paths of steadfast love and faithfulness. It is right to share our blessings in a world where justice for many is still but a dream, and mercy is but a hope seen from afar. With thankful hearts, let us joyfully share our gifts in gratitude to our God.

Offering Prayer (1 Thess 3)

How can we thank you enough, Blessed One,
> for all you have given us.

May we increase and enrich in love,
> even as you increase and enrich the gifts
> > we bring before you this day.

Send them forth into your world,
> as signs of the bounty of Christ
> > coming into the world.

In your precious name, we pray. Amen.

Sending Forth

Benediction (1 Thess 3)
> May your love for one another abound,
>> just as Christ's love abounds for you.
>
> Go with God's love in your hearts
>> and with the Spirit's fierce tenderness
>> in your breast.
>
> Go with God.

December 5, 2021

Second Sunday of Advent
Deborah Sokolove

Color

Purple

Scripture Readings

Malachi 3:1-4; Luke 1:68-79; Philippians 1:3-11; Luke 3:1-6

Theme Ideas

God sends messengers to remind us that the Holy One is always on the side of peace, justice, mercy, and loving kindness. These prophets speak of a day when light will be given to all who live in darkness and despair. Now is the time to prepare the way for this promised day in which God will live among us, and everyone will see the salvation of God.

Invitation and Gathering

Centering Words (Luke 1)

By the tender mercy of our God, the dawn from on high will break upon us—giving light to those who sit in darkness, comforting those who dwell in the shadow of death, and guiding our feet in the way of peace.

Call to Worship (Mal 3, Luke 3:4)
A messenger calls, "Prepare the way of the Holy One.
Make a pathway for God straight into your hearts."
Blessed be the Holy One,
who brings light into the deepest shadows.
A prophet proclaims, "Make way in the desert
for the coming of God to live in our midst."
Blessed be the Holy One,
who comes to live among us in peace.
Are you ready for the coming Day of God?
Let us worship the one who calls us into light.

Opening Prayer (Mal 3, Luke 3)
Redeeming Keeper of Promises,
your messengers remind us
that you are the source of peace, justice, mercy,
and loving kindness.
As we prepare for your coming in your Son Jesus,
help us shine as the radiant body of Christ,
that we may be light for a gloomy, broken world.
Amen.

Proclamation and Response

Prayer of Confession (Mal 3, Luke 3)
God of light and love, your prophets call us
to prepare for your coming,
and to open our hearts to all
who seek compassion and relief.
Too often, we close our ears to cries of pain,
closing ourselves off from the healing power
of kindness and love.

Your messengers call us to straighten the paths
of all who might stumble,
and to make a way in the wilderness,
where there seems to be no way at all.
Too often, we close our eyes
to the sight of those in need,
fearing that justice for others
will bring loss to ourselves.
You call us to bring light into the shadowy places,
and to be messengers of your coming
into a world of death and despair.
Forgive us when we are unwilling to bear your light,
when we close off the pathways of our hearts
to those who are in need of your good news.

Words of Assurance (Luke 1)
Hear the good news:
When we cannot find our way through the gloom,
God gives light to those who sit in darkness
and in the shadow of death,
to guide our feet into the way of peace.
In the name of Jesus Christ, you are forgiven.
In the name of Jesus Christ, you are forgiven.
Glory to God. Amen.

Passing the Peace of Christ (Luke 1)
As we prepare to welcome Jesus as the light of the world,
let us share light with one another with signs of peace.
The peace of Christ be with you.
The peace of Christ be with you always.

Prayer of Preparation (Luke 1, Luke 3)
Eternal Light of the world,
you have promised to live among us,
to save your people from fear, oppression,
and death.

Open our hearts to the wisdom of your holy Word,
that we may see and hear and feel your presence
in our lives. Amen.

Response to the Word (Luke 1, Luke 3)
Indwelling Light of our hearts,
we have heard your voice
in the words of your messengers.
We give thanks that you are Immanuel,
God with us.

Thanksgiving and Communion

Offering Prayer (Luke 1)
Immanuel, God with us, in gratitude for the mercy
you showed our ancestors in faith,
and in thanksgiving for your holy covenant
with all your people,
we offer you these gifts and offerings.
Amen.

Great Thanksgiving
Christ be with you.
And also with you.
Lift up your hearts.
We lift them up to God.
Let us give our thanks to the Holy One.
It is right to give our thanks and praise.

It is a right, good, and joyful thing
always and everywhere to give our thanks to you,
who sent the prophet Malachi
to announce your coming reign,

the priest Zechariah
to remind us of your tender mercy,
and John the Baptist
to proclaim your coming among us in Jesus.
You promise to give light to all who are in despair,
and to guide our feet on the way of peace.

And so, with your creatures on earth
and all the heavenly chorus,
we praise your name and join their unending hymn:
Holy, holy, holy Lord, God of power and might,
heaven and earth are full of your glory.
Hosanna in the highest. Blessed is the one
who comes in the name of the Lord.
Hosanna in the highest.

Holy are you, and holy is your child, Jesus Christ,
whose birth in our hearts we prepare
with hope and anticipation,
and for whose life, passion, death, and resurrection
we give thanks beyond measure.

On the night in which he gave himself up,
Jesus took bread, broke it, saying:
"Take, eat, all of you.
This is my body, broken for you.
Whenever you eat it,
do so in remembrance of me."
After supper, he took the cup, saying:
"This is the cup of the new covenant,
poured out for the healing of the world.

Whenever you drink it,
do so in remembrance of me."

And so, in remembrance of your mighty acts
in Jesus Christ, we proclaim the mystery of faith.
Christ has died.
Christ is risen.
Christ will come again.

Pour out your Holy Spirit on us,
and on these gifts of bread and wine.
Make them be for us the body and blood of Christ,
that we may be the body of Christ
to a world that sits too often in gloom and fear.
Creator of all, Light of the world, Spirit of truth,
you are the one God to whom we offer our praise
and our thanks. Amen.

Sending Forth

Benediction (Phil 1)
As we await the coming of the Promised One,
may your love and knowledge
and insight overflow,
that you may live in peace and harmony
with all beings for the glory and praise of God.
Amen.

December 12, 2021

Third Sunday of Advent

B. J. Beu
Copyright © B. J. Beu

Color

Purple

Scripture Readings

Zephaniah 3:14-20; Isaiah 12:2-6; Philippians 4:4-7;
Luke 3:7-18

Theme Ideas

God's salvation is at hand. Philippians captures the
mood of the day: "Rejoice in the Lord always; again I
will say, Rejoice" (4:4 NRSV). Isaiah and Zephaniah invite us to sing aloud and shout for joy. Through God, the
warrior receives victory while the lame and outcast no
longer live in shame. Three of today's lections celebrate
the joy of our salvation—but the Gospel lesson reminds
us that salvation demands more than our joy. Beyond
calling sinners to repent, John the Baptist warns of the
wrath to come for those who hear the good news and
reject it. Justice is the order of the day. Salvation entails
judgment, and we need to be ready.

Invitation and Gathering

Centering Words (Phil 4:4 NRSV)
> "Rejoice in the Lord always; again I will say, Rejoice."

Call to Worship (Zeph 3, Isa 12, Phil 4)
> Let all who love God rejoice.
> > **Let all who thirst for justice**
> > **draw water from the well of God's salvation.**
>
> Let all who long for Christ sing for joy.
> > **Let all who hunger for righteousness**
> > **return home to the living God.**
>
> Let all who seek the Spirit shout aloud.
> > **Let all who yearn for mercy**
> > **fall on their knees before the throne of grace.**

Opening Prayer (Zeph 3, Isa 12)
> God of our salvation, you bring victory to the righteous
> > and comfort to the outcast.
>
> As we come before you this day,
> > lighten our hearts with laughter
> > > and loosen our tongues to sing your praise.
>
> For you alone are the source of our hope;
> > you alone are the fountain of our joy.
>
> Be with us now and always. Amen.

Proclamation and Response

Prayer of Yearning (Zeph 3, Isa 12, Phil 4)
> Source of compassion and grace,
> > we yearn to embody the joy of your salvation,
> > > but we are easily distracted
> > > > by the demands of the season;
> > we long to taste the wellspring of your mercy,
> > > but we are caught up in the frenzy of the holidays.

Be our quiet center,
    that we may find your joy deep within.
Be our secret heart,
    that we may live lives of love
        wherever we go.
In your holy name, we pray. Amen.

Words of Assurance (Zeph 3, Luke 3)

The one who loves us with a fierce tenderness
    takes away our guilt and leads us in the ways of life.
The one who guides us with justice and mercy
    restores our fortunes and leads us home.

Passing the Peace of Christ

The joy of this season is found in simple moments of warmth and caring. Let us demonstrate the joy we have discovered in this church by passing the peace of Christ with one another.

Introduction to the Word (Zeph 3)

Let all who wish to know the ways of life and death listen for the word of God. Truly, the presence of the Lord is in this place.

Response to the Word (Isa 12)

Give thanks to the Lord.
    Call on God's holy name.
Make known God's deeds among the peoples.
    Sing praises to our God,
    who is worthy of our praise.
Great is the God of Israel.
    God is greatly to be praised.

Thanksgiving and Communion

Offering Prayer
> Generous God, the bounty of your love
>> overflows into every aspect of our lives.
>
> May the gifts we bring before you this day
>> be a sign of our commitment to share our love
>>> with those in need.
>
> May the offerings we place upon your Lord's table
>> symbolize our trust in your power to heal the world
>>> through the works of our hands
>>>> and the ministries of your church.
>
> In Christ's name, we pray. Amen.

Sending Forth

Benediction (Phil 4)
> Go with the joy of the Lord on your lips.
> Go with the peace of Christ in your hearts.
> Go with the strength of the Holy Spirit
>> in every step you take.
> Go with God.

December 19, 2021

Fourth Sunday of Advent

B. J. Beu

Color

Purple

Scripture Readings

Micah 5:2-5a; Luke 1:47-55; Hebrews 10:5-10;
Luke 1:30-45, (46-55)

Theme Ideas

Today's scriptures are filled with joyous expectation.
Micah proclaims that a joyous hope will come forth
from Bethlehem—one who will bring gifts of security,
peace, nurture, and strength for the people. Elizabeth receives Mary's visit with joyous expectation, as her baby
leaps in her womb and she is filled with the Holy Spirit.
Receiving Elizabeth's blessing in return, Mary expresses
joyous expectation for the child she carries for the world.
Christmas is a time to be pregnant with expectation and
joy. It is a time to receive anew the miraculous blessings
that come when joyous expectations are fulfilled.

Invitation and Gathering

Centering Words (Luke 1)

The very air we breathe is filled with joyous expectation. The one who has done great things for us is with us now. Glory to God in the highest!

Call to Worship (Luke 1)

When Mary visited her cousin Elizabeth,
their lives were forever changed.
> **Elizabeth was filled with the Holy Spirit**
> **and Mary proclaimed faith in God, her savior.**
The children they carried in their wombs
heralded expectation and hope for the world.
> **We are heirs of this expectation and hope.**
> **We are heirs of this promise of God.**
Come! Let us worship.

Opening Prayer (Luke 1)

God of joyous expectation, come to us this day.
May the miracles in our lives fill us with wonder.
May an encounter with your goodness and grace
    cause our hearts to leap within us.
Receive us into the arms of your mercy,
    that we may feel you near us
        and rest secure in your many blessings. Amen.

Proclamation and Response

Prayer of Yearning (Luke 1)

It is hard to wait patiently, O God,
    for the gift of your promised salvation.

We long to nurture the joyous expectation
    that Mary and Elizabeth discovered in their greeting,
        but we have grown accustomed
            to living with disappointment.
We yearn to feel our hearts leap within us
    as your Spirit stirs our slumbering souls,
        but we have allowed ourselves
            to find solace in lesser things.
Fill us with your grace,
    that we may give birth to hope and joy,
        and that we may abide in your peace and love.
In Christ's name, we pray. Amen.

Words of Assurance (Luke 1)

Do not let your hearts be troubled.
God will not fail to lift you out of complacency
    and fill your hearts to overflowing.
Rise in joy and hope,
    for God's promises are sure,
    and Christ's salvation is at hand.

Passing the Peace of Christ (Mic 5, Luke 1)

To be followers of Christ is to share the peace he brought
into the world. Let us share signs of this love and peace
with one another as beloved children of God.

Introduction to the Word (Luke 1)

While Mary and Elizabeth were pregnant with very
different sons, they shared a joyous expectation for the
miracles of God growing within them. As we hear their
stories, let us listen with expectation and hope for the
miracles that God is birthing within us.

Response to the Word (Luke 1)

The God of Israel is our source of hope.
Glory to God in the highest.
The God of our fathers is our source of strength.
Glory to God in the highest.
The God of our mothers is our source of courage.
Glory to God in the highest.
The God of Jesus Christ is our source of love and light.
Glory to God in the highest.

Thanksgiving and Communion

Invitation to the Offering (Mic 5)

Those who keep God's covenant and decrees walk in the paths of steadfast love and faithfulness. It is right to share our blessing in a world where justice for many is but a dream, and mercy is but a hope seen from afar. With thankful hearts, let us joyfully share our gifts in gratitude to our God.

Offering Prayer (Luke 1)

Glorious God, source of every good gift,
bless our tithes and offerings this day.
May they lift up the lowly,
fill the hungry with good things,
and bring strength and mercy
to those in need.
In your holy name, we pray. Amen.

Sending Forth

Benediction (Luke 1)

Go forth and bear Christ's hope to the world.

We will carry Christ's hope everywhere we go.

Go forth and bear the mystery of God before others.

We will shine God's light each and every day.

Go forth and bless the world.

**We will share the Spirit in all that we say
and in all that we do.**

December 24, 2021

Christmas Eve

Mary Scifres

Color

White

Scripture Readings

Isaiah 9:2-7; Psalm 96; Titus 2:11-14; Luke 2:1-20

Theme Ideas

Everything turns around on this night of nights. The Light of the World arrives in the humblest of circumstances, and angels proclaim glory to the humblest of servants. Light breaks into the darkest of times, and yokes of oppression are shattered to free the enslaved. A child becomes the savior proclaimed by centuries of prophets bringing good news for all people, and for creation itself. Even the trees will break forth in song, for everything turns around on this night called Christmas Eve.

Invitation and Gathering

Centering Words (Isa 9, Luke 2)

A child cries out. New life begins, hope is born, and light shines forth for all to see.

Call to Worship (Isa 9, Luke 2)

Rejoice and sing.

A child is born!

Sing songs of praise.

For the Prince of Peace is in our midst.

Rejoice and sing.

Christ is born! Hallelujah. Amen.

Opening Prayer or Response to the Word (Isa 9, Titus 2, Luke 2)

Wonderful Counselor, Mighty God,

be born in our hearts this night.

Shine your light into the darkness of our world,

that all the earth might know your glorious presence

and that all people might find hope

in your love and grace.

In your glorious name, we pray. Amen.

Proclamation and Response

Prayer of Confession (Isa 9, Titus 2, Luke 2)

When the shadows of sin and sorrow surround us,

shine on us with the light of your comfort

and your grace.

When the despair of the world overwhelms us,

lift us with your promise of hope.

When we forget the good news of your presence,

cry out with your message of love,

that we might hear and remember anew.

Christ is born.

Christ is with us.

We are not alone.

In your beloved name, we pray. Amen.

Words of Assurance (Isa 9, Titus 2)
> We are not alone.
> We who were walking in darkness
> > have seen a great light.
> Light has dawned, and the grace of God has appeared,
> > bringing salvation to us, salvation to all.
> Thanks be to God.

Passing the Peace of Christ (Isa 9, Titus 2)
> As the Prince of Peace has blessed us with grace, so now we are invited to bless one another with Christ's message of peace.
> > Peace be with you.
> > **And also with you.**

Introduction to the Word or Response to the Word (Luke 2)
> May we, like Mary before us, treasure these words and ponder them in our hearts.

Thanksgiving and Communion

Invitation to the Offering (Matt 2, Luke 2)
> Kings brought gifts. Angels sang praise. Shepherds told tales. Every gift we have to offer the Christ child is a precious gift, blessed by God. Bring your gifts. Bring your hearts. Bring your lives, in gratitude and celebration of the Christ child whose birth we celebrate this night.

Offering Prayer (Isa 9, Titus 2, Luke 2)
> Beautiful Savior, we are so grateful for your birth
> > so many years ago,
> > > and we are so joyful
> > > > to have your presence in our lives this night.

In gratitude, we offer our gifts,
    however humble they might be.
Transform our gifts with your glory and grace,
    that our gifts might become grace and love,
        and light and hope,
            for a world in need of you. Amen.

Sending Forth

Benediction (Isa 9, Titus 2, Luke 2)
    Go forth and shine light in the darkness.
    Go and bring peace into our troubled world.
    Proclaim hope in the midst of despair.
    Go with God's blessings—
        for a child has been born to us,
        who is Love for the nations
        and Light for the world. Amen.

December 26, 2021

First Sunday after Christmas Day
Laura Jaquith Bartlett

Color

White

Scripture Readings

1 Samuel 2:18-20, 26; Psalm 148; Colossians 3:12-17;
Luke 2:41-52

Theme Ideas

Well, it's the day after Christmas and Jesus is
now…twelve years old? Where does the time go?! Ac-
tually, that question is at the heart of how we structure
our liturgical calendar, year in and year out. We know
that Jesus grows to be a curious and wise twelve-year-
old, and then a compassionate and prophetic adult, and
then a radical and redemptive savior, but we need to
take time to rehearse and relive those stories every year
in order to rehearse and relive our response. May we
sing with the angels, clothe ourselves with love, and
make sure that *everything* we do is in the name of Christ
Jesus.

Invitation and Gathering

Centering Words (1 Sam 2, Ps 148, Col 3, Luke 2)

Christmas comes, Christmas goes…but God's love is everlasting. Babies are born, babies grow up…but God's love is everlasting. The God who made the entire world is with us here and now, and forever and ever. Alleluia!

Call to Worship (Ps 148, Col 3, Luke 2)

God's love has come to earth to dwell with us.
Sing for joy with the angels.
We are God's chosen people, loved and cherished.
Sing for joy with the angels.
The birth of Love has changed us forever.
Sing for joy with the angels.
Let us sing, praise, rejoice, and worship together!

Opening Prayer (1 Sam 2, Col 3, Luke 2)

(Consider singing the first stanza of "Love Came Down at Christmas" [United Methodist Hymnal #242] as a response; the music could be playing quietly underneath the spoken prayer.)

God of the Incarnation, even as we celebrate
the Love that was born at Christmas,
we know that your love continues to grow
far beyond Christmas Day.
Even as parents watch tenderly and proudly
as their children grow into adulthood,
you hold us in your compassionate embrace
throughout our lives.

Guide us into mature faith, O God,
>that we might be like Jesus in our love,
>>in our humility and wisdom,
>>>and in every word and deed.
Shape us, inspire us, challenge us,
>and bless us with the music to sing your praises.
Amen.

Proclamation and Response

Prayer of Confession (1 Sam 2, Ps 148, Col 3, Luke 2)
God, you are the Parent of all creation.
You know what it is to love your children passionately.
And you know how it feels
>when your children turn away.
We, your children, love you passionately,
>but we have also turned away.
Sometimes we act like spoiled brats.
Sometimes we turn our back on you.
Sometimes we pretend we don't need a parent anymore.
God, forgive us.
Feed us with the bread of heaven.
Teach us with your wisdom.
Tell us your stories.
Dress us once more in the clothing of your love,
>that we may sing your praises in perfect harmony.
Alleluia!

Words of Assurance (Col 3)

(Divide the congregation into two parts.)
You are God's chosen ones, holy and beloved!
God has already forgiven you.
You are God's chosen ones, holy and beloved!
God has already forgiven you.
Thanks be to God!
Alleluia!

Passing the Peace of Christ (Col 3)

As God's chosen ones, we are to let the peace of Christ rule in our hearts, because we are one body. We are also to be thankful. So I invite you to pass the peace with these words:
"May the peace of Christ rule in your heart."
And the response will be:
"I am thankful."

Response to the Word (Col 3, Luke 2)

(The music for "Dona Nobis Pacem" [United Methodist Hymnal #376] could play underneath.)
Swaddled in a manger, Jesus is born.
Clothed with love, we sing Christ's peace.
Growing in faith, Jesus finds his place
among the wise ones.
Teaching one another, we sing Christ's peace.
Called by God, Jesus offers us healing and love.
Called by God, we sing Christ's peace.
With the peace of Christ in our hearts,
let us sing in God's perfect harmony.
(If this response is led by three people, have voices 1, 2, and 3 lead their sections, starting one at a time, in singing "Dona Nobis Pacem" in canon.)

Thanksgiving and Communion

Invitation to the Offering (Luke 2)

Can you imagine how relieved and grateful Joseph and Mary were when they finally found Jesus safely in the temple? And now we have found Jesus right here in our own worship space! Mary treasured the experience in her heart. We have our own Jesus experiences to treasure in our hearts. Out of that gratitude, that extreme joy, comes the desire to offer our gifts. Let us rejoice together as we share today's offering.

Offering Prayer (Col 3)

God of miracles, when Jesus was born,
>   angels, shepherds, sages, and even animals
>   rejoiced and gave thanks.
Today, we delight in our chance
>   to join the Christmas party of gratitude.
Thank you for naming us your beloved children.
We offer you our hearts, our deeds, and our entire lives
>   in thanksgiving for the gift of Christ Jesus,
>   in whose name we pray. Amen.

Sending Forth

Benediction

(Led by two speakers.)
You are God's chosen ones, holy and beloved.
>   *So clothe yourselves with compassion, kindness,*
>   *humility, meekness, patience, and love.*
You have been called into the one body,
where the peace of Christ is the ruler.
>   *So be thankful, and join the song of the angels.*

You live in the richness of Christ's word
with wisdom and music all around.
>   *So teach others the Way of Christ.*
And whatever you do,
>   *in word,*
or in deed,
>   *do everything,*
everything,
>   *in the name of the Lord Jesus Christ.*
Go in Christ's peace to serve God and your neighbor.
>   *Amen.*

Contributors

Laura Jaquith Bartlett is an ordained deacon with a passion for music and worship, who serves in The United Methodist Church's Oregon-Idaho annual conference. She is the immediate past president of The Fellowship of United Methodists in Music & Worship Arts, and was the Worship and Music Director for the UMC's 2016 General Conference.

B. J. Beu is a pastor, spiritual director, and coach who has served churches in the United Church of Christ for over twenty-five years. B. J. lives in Laguna Beach with his wife, Mary, and their son, Michael, when he is not at California State University Northridge studying film.

Susan Blain is Minister for Worship, Liturgy, and Spiritual Formation with Local Church Ministries of the United Church of Christ. Sue works with writers and liturgists from around the UCC to create *Worship Ways*, the online resource for lectionary-based worship. She edited volumes 2 and 3 of *Imaging the Word: An Arts and Lectionary Resource* (© 1995 and 1996 United Church Press). She served on the editorial board for *Sing! Prayer and Praise* (© 2009 Pilgrim Press).

Mary Petrina Boyd is pastor of Langley United Methodist Church on Whidbey Island. She spends alternating summers working as an archaeologist in Jordan.

Joanne Carlson Brown is a United Methodist minister serving Tibbetts UMC in West Seattle, Washington. She lives with her *anam cara*, Christie, and Thistle, the Wonder Westie.

James Dollins is Senior Pastor of Anaheim United Methodist Church in Southern California, where he lives with his wife, Serena, and sons, Forrest and Silas. He is a lover of music, intercultural ministries, and God's creation.

Karin Ellis is a United Methodist pastor who lives with her husband and children in Tustin, California. She enjoys writing liturgy for worship and writing children's stories.

Rebecca J. Kruger Gaudino, a United Church of Christ minister in Portland, Oregon, teaches biblical studies and theology at the University of Portland and also writes for the church.

Bill Hoppe is the music coordinator and keyboardist for Bear Creek United Methodist Church in Woodinville, Washington, and is a friend of Aslan.

Kirsten Linford grew up in Red Rock Christian Church in Boise, Idaho, and has strong Disciples roots. She is currently the pastor of Westwood Hills Congregational Church (UCC) in Los Angeles. Active in both the Disciples and UCC churches, she has served on committees at both the association/conference and national levels. Kirsten shares her life with her young daughter, Riley, and their golden retriever, Seamus.

Joanne Reynolds is a hymn poet who worships with Congregational churches that are members of the United

Church of Christ—Corona del Mar, California; Crested Butte, Colorado; and Scituate, Massachusetts.

Bob Rhodes is a "cradle Methodist," now serving as Lead Pastor at Pacific Beach United Methodist Church in San Diego, California. Bob's passions include technology, music, family, and God.

Karen Clark Ristine is a journalist turned United Methodist minister and is also an editor, writer, preacher, and fan girl of the Holy Spirit.

Mary Scifres is a United Methodist pastor, motivational speaker, teacher, and author who brings both inspiration and expertise for twenty-first-century leadership in creative worship, church growth, change management, visioning, and strategic planning. Learn more at www.mary scifres.com.

Deborah Sokolove is Professor of Art and Worship at Wesley Theological Seminary, where she also serves as the Director of the Henry Luce III Center for the Arts and Religion.

Michelle L. Torigian is a pastor in the United Church of Christ and blogs at michelletorigian.com.